The Golden Throne

CHRISTOPHER de BELLAIGUE

The Golden Throne

The Curse of a King

THE BODLEY HEAD
LONDON

1 3 5 7 9 10 8 6 4 2

The Bodley Head, an imprint of Vintage, is part of
the Penguin Random House group of companies

Vintage, Penguin Random House UK,
One Embassy Gardens, 8 Viaduct Gardens,
London SW11 7BW

penguin.co.uk/vintage
global.penguinrandomhouse.com

Penguin
Random House
UK

First published by The Bodley Head in 2025

Copyright © Christopher de Bellaigue 2025

Christopher de Bellaigue has asserted his right to be identified as the author of this
Work in accordance with the Copyright, Designs and Patents Act 1988

Maps by Michael A. Hill
Illustrations by Melchior Lorck (c. 1527–83) from *Melchior Lorck*
by Erik Fischer, The Royal Library, Vandkunsten Publishers, Copenhagen, 2009

Typeset in 11.5/15pt Sabon LT Std by Jouve (UK), Milton Keynes
Printed and bound in Great Britain by Clays Ltd, Elcograf S.p.A.

The authorised representative in the EEA is Penguin Random House Ireland,
Morrison Chambers, 32 Nassau Street, Dublin D02 YH68

A CIP catalogue record for this book is available from the British Library

HB ISBN 9781847927422
TPB ISBN 9781847927439

Penguin Random House is committed to a sustainable future
for our business, our readers and our planet. This book is made
from Forest Stewardship Council® certified paper.

For my father

Contents

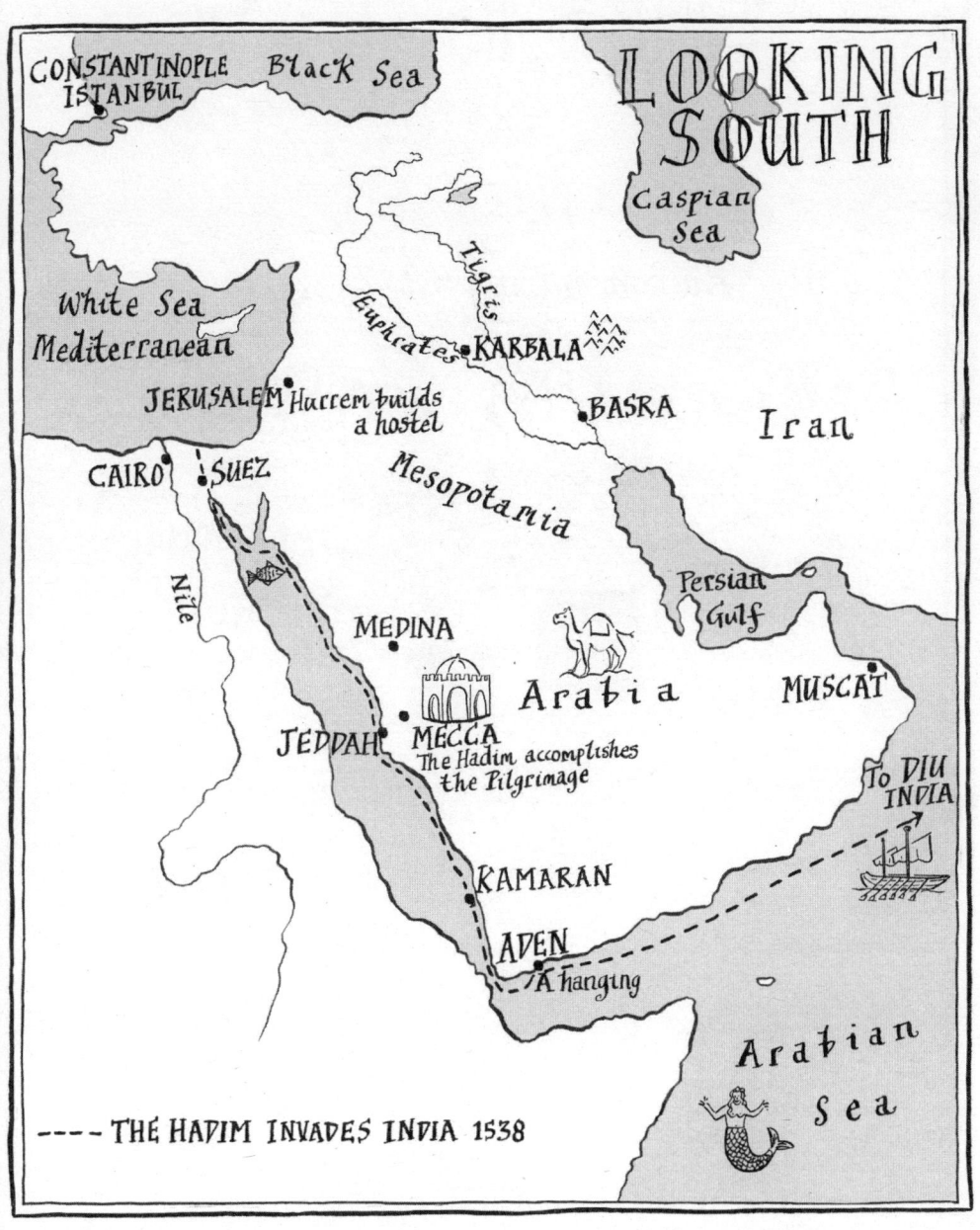

CONSTANTINOPLE
ISTANBUL

Black Sea

LOOKING SOUTH

Caspian Sea

White Sea
Mediterranean

Euphrates

Tigris

KARBALA

JERUSALEM

Hurrem builds
a hostel

BASRA

Iran

CAIRO

SUEZ

Mesopotamia

Nile

MEDINA

Arabia

Persian
Gulf

MUSCAT

JEDDAH

MECCA
The Hadim accomplishes
the Pilgrimage

To DIU
INDIA

KAMARAN

ADEN

A hanging

Arabian

Sea

----- THE HADIM INVADES INDIA 1538

LOOKING WEST

Austria

VIENNA

Danube

Rincon intercepted
Po
VENICE

France GENOA
REGGIO
Hayreddin weds Maria

NICE

ELBA
TALAMONE

TOULON
The fleet winters
PORTO ERCOLE
ROME

SARDINIA

LIPARI
A shameful episode

Storm
ALGIERS
Sicily

–·–·– MOLDAVIAN CAMPAIGN 1538

––––– HAYREDDIN'S RAZZIA 1544

····· CHARLES'S ASSAULT ON ALGIERS 1541

Carpathians
BUDA
Hungary
SUCEAVA
'The Golden Throne'
BENDER
Brother George defenestrated
ALBA IULIA
Pruit
Transylvania
BELGRADE
Serbia
Wallachia
Danube
SARAJEVO
Rustem's Birthplace
Black Sea
EDIRNE
ISTANBUL
CONSTANTINOPLE
Albania
CORFU
MANISA
PREVESA
The wind dies
The Morea
CHIOS
Rhodes
White Sea
Mediterranean

Crimea

Black Sea

ISTANBUL, CONSTANTINOPLE

USKUDAR

AMASYA

Animal arm
ERZINCAI

GEYIKLI BABA
Prince Selim
becomes heir
apparent

PHRYGIA

Anatolia

KONYA
Birthplace of Sinan

EREGLI

Rhodes

ALEPPO
Big Hunt

Syria

White Sea
Mediterranean

Egypt

•••••• SULEYMAN'S IRAN CAMPAIGN 1548
------ ALQAS MIRZA'S DEPREDATIONS 1548

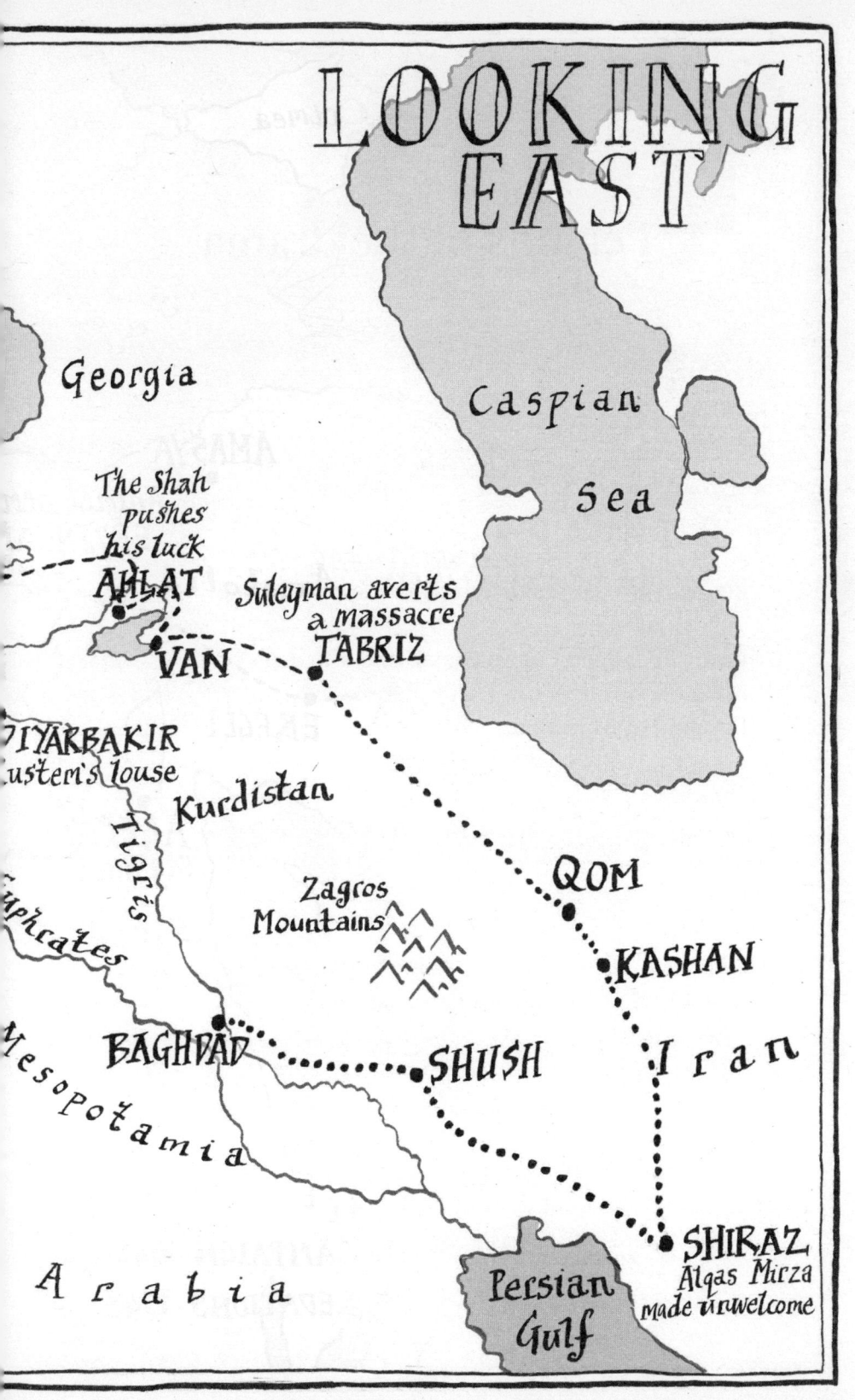

LOOKING EAST

Georgia

Caspian Sea

The Shah pushes his luck
AHLAT

VAN

Suleyman averts a massacre
TABRIZ

DIYARBAKIR
Rustem's louse

Kurdistan

Tigris

Euphrates

Zagros Mountains

QOM

KASHAN

Iran

BAGHDAD

SHUSH

Mesopotamia

Arabia

Persian Gulf

SHIRAZ
Alqas Mirza made unwelcome

Persons of the drama

The Ottomans
Suleyman I, tenth Sultan of the Ottomans

Hurrem, Ruthenian consort of the Sultan,
   known variously as the Haseki or Special Friend,
   and Roxelana
Mihrimah, daughter of Suleyman and Hurrem   The Cabal
Rustem the Bosnian, former pig driver,
   husband of Mihrimah

Mehmet
Selim   sons of Suleyman and Hurrem
Bayezit
Cihangir

Mahidevran, former consort of the Sultan, rival to Hurrem
Mustafa, son of Mahidevran and Suleyman

Suleyman Pasha, known as the Hadim, a eunuch
Hayreddin Barbarossa, Captain Pasha or head of the
   Ottoman navy
Hassan, his protégé, Governor of Algiers
Lutfi Pasha, brother-in-law to Suleyman, vizier
Sah Sultan, Suleyman's sister and patron to

Merkez Efendi, a divine
Yahya, a dervish
Sinan, an architect
Ebussuud Efendi, Mufti or chief religious authority

Mehmet II, Suleyman's great-grandfather, Conqueror of Istanbul
Bayezit II, Sulyeman's grandfather, eighth Ottoman Sultan
Selim I, Suleyman's father, ninth Ottoman Sultan

The Christians
Martin Luther, a reformer
Charles V, King of Spain and Holy Roman Emperor
Ferdinand, Archduke of Austria and Bohemia, Charles's
    younger brother, known also as the King of the Romans
Maria, regent of the Netherlands, their sister

Francis I, King of France, known as the Most Christian King

Antonio Rincon   Francis's diplomats
Captain Polin

Johann Maria Malvezzi
Gerard Veltwyck   Hapsburg diplomats
Jerome Laski

John Sigismund, intended King of Hungary
Isabella, Dowager Queen of Hungary, his mother
George Martinuzzi, Bishop of Oradea, known as Brother
    George, regent of Hungary

The Iranians
Tahmasp, Shah of Iran
Alqas Mirza, his brother
Ulama, a turncoat

Act One: A House Divided

I

Francis of France is a most kingly king. Even if you saw him without his jewels and gold brocade, so noble and majestic are his movements that you would say: here is the King. He is called the Most Christian King because he was anointed with the sacred chrism, the oil which God sent down from heaven to show his affection for France.

It is eight hundred years since the Muslim advance into France was checked at the Battle of Tours. Over subsequent centuries parish vaults across the kingdom have been filled with the tombs of French Crusaders. In our own time Erasmus of Rotterdam has described France as the 'purest . . . part of Christendom', the streets of Paris full of theological students and the Sorbonne renowned for its defence of the faith. Not for nothing is France known as the eldest daughter of the Church of Rome. And now, in the autumn of 1534, she is receiving a dozen Turkish gentlemen.

They were conveyed across the Mediterranean on individual galleys for fear of interception by the Emperor's fleet. They wear immaculate turbans and drink nothing but water. The gossips say that they have come to find a good French wife for the Sultan, who is resolved on baptism for himself and one of his sons. But more considered opinion is troubled by Francis's embrace of a heathen enemy who grows bolder by the year.

Francis defends his policy to the ambassador of the Most

Serene Republic of Venice. 'I strongly desire to see the Turk all-powerful and ready for war,' he says, 'not for his sake, for he is an infidel, and we are Christian, but to enfeeble the Emperor's might [and] put him to heavy expense'. And he points out that other Christian nations live in peace with the Turk – a reference to the Serenissima herself. The King will not be deterred from his objective of a pact with the Sultan against the Emperor and sealed with Turkish cash. But it would help if he could show his critics what a good Catholic he is.

One night the Lutherans, who have become very insolent of late, creep around Paris putting up placards in prominent places that the faithful see on their way to church. 'True articles on the horrible, great and insufferable abuses of the papal Mass,' as the tract is called, takes an axe to the taproot of Catholic devotion. It describes transubstantiation, by which the bread and wine of the Blessed Sacrament become the body and blood of Christ, as an 'execrable blasphemy' and the priests who preside over this ritual as 'false antichrists'.

One can always tell when Francis is feeling emotional because his eyes, which are hard to ignore in the first place, being permanently bloodshot, roll upwards. Such a rolling presumably occurs on the November morning when he emerges from his bedchamber to find that someone has pinned a copy of the 'True articles' to his door. But this is the opportunity he has been waiting for.

Justice flows swiftly and on 13 November a shoemaker's son, who spent his youth in dissolution before he was completely paralysed, apart from his tongue which he used to propagate the heresy, is burned alive at the cemetery of Saint-Jean. The following day it is the turn of a rich draper, at the same cemetery, but not before his hand is cut off for the edification of a crowd outside Notre Dame. Other casualties include a schoolmistress who obligingly gives the names of other members of her sect before she too subsides beneath the flames.

Perhaps it is the strange passions that have been released, or the savour of human fat on the cold air, but still Paris doesn't settle. Rumours of a massacre abound. A Flemish merchant is murdered on suspicion of being German. Then, on the night of 13 January 1535, the heretics plant another screed.

Something must be done.

~

It is as if all of Paris is in the procession that sets out on 21 January from the church of Saint-Germain or in the crowds that gather to watch.

First come representatives of the parishes of the city, each with his banner and cross, then the merchants and the well-to-do holding lighted torches and marching in pairs along the crest of the road, all in excellent order. They are followed by the four mendicant orders in their gowns and chasubles, and the priests and canons of the churches, many of them barefoot.

They and the monks from the city's monasteries carry the remains of saints in reliquaries chased in gold and inlaid with precious stones, but not as precious as the treasures within. Six priests bear the head of King Louis, who died while crusading at Tunis and whose ribs, arms and shanks have been distributed to churches throughout Christendom.

The most precious relic in Paris is the Crown of Thorns worn by Christ on his final journey and the sight of it causes the hairs of the people to stand on end. Then come bishops, archbishops and cardinals, again in pairs, carrying iron from the lance that pierced Christ's side, the napkins of his babyhood and the tablet of stone which the children of Israel hewed in the desert.

If by adoring relics one can enter heaven, the people of Paris have a head start. And since the Lutherans so abhor the Blessed Sacrament, the Blessed Sacrament is what they shall have. Here it is, carried by the Bishop of Paris, under a canopy of crimson velvet that is hoisted on poles held by the Dauphin, his younger brothers the Duke of Orleans and the Duke of Angouleme and another grandee, a pole apiece.

Behind them, dressed in black, his smooth, neatly combed brown hair shown to best effect, walks the Most Christian King.

The majesty of the occasion is complemented by the excellence of his construction, his tall, well-built frame, his muscular buttocks and thighs, his skin the colour of watery milk. When the procession stops and the Blessed Sacrament is placed on an altar in the street, someone in the crowd calls, 'Sire, do good justice!' To which the King replies with a sign indicating that this is his intention.

After Mass at Notre-Dame he makes a speech in which he urges his subjects to denounce all heretics, even if they are close relatives. The day ends with six more public burnings and the King's Muslim guests are escorted past pyres being fed Christians by other Christians.

~

One can fight against the Turks or do deals with them. With the Lutherans things are less straightforward. They are part of the body of the Church and cannot be cut out without killing it.

In Germany the heresy is no longer confined to the ignorant masses, a matter of sermons interrupted and altarpieces defiled. Every day princes, nobles and substantial citizens go over, crying 'Luther!' and 'Death to the Pope!' Before he left Rome in February 1535 the Pope's envoy Pietro Paolo Vergerio warned the cardinals of this state of affairs – not that they seemed very concerned, being occupied with their own pleasures and self-interest. He even spoke with Pope Paul himself, who was good enough to invite him to his hunting lodge between the city and the sea. And Paul agreed with Vergerio on the need for a council to set the heretics straight, ordering him north to lay the groundwork.

Since reaching Germany Vergerio has done everything he can to avoid Luther's hometown of Wittenberg. But if you're going from Halle to Berlin to confer with the Elector of Brandenburg it's in the way. So here he is, in November of that same year, 1535, sitting to breakfast in lodgings a few yards from the church door to which Luther pinned his so-called theses, the gate where he burned the Papal bull of excommunication and the university where he peddles his lies, when the scourge of Christ walks in.

Martin Luther wears a surcoat with satin sleeves and a fur-lined serge robe, a curiously festive look that he rounds off with rings and a heavy gold pendant. He seems a decade younger than his forty years and is plumper than the portraits. But the essentials that everyone knows, the bold cheekbones and lips, the walnut chin and the kiss-curl springing like lichen over a lump of head, are unmistakable.

Well this is awkward.

The Pope's representatives are trained not to raise their voices or betray shock and dismay. But nothing has prepared Vergerio for the fox that is destroying the vineyard to leer over his break-fast and say, in a voice both soft and taunting, 'tell me, over there in Italy have you heard something of my reputation for being a German drunk?'

Vergerio stays silent, which Luther interprets as an invitation to talk. He only needs one. He boasts that his Katie has given him five children, two females and three males, and that his twelve-year-old shows every sign of becoming a great preacher. Then he mentions that he is entertaining a doctor of the law sent by King Henry of England. This is the same Henry who recently usurped the Pope's authority, unlawfully divorced his wife Catherine of Aragon – the Emperor's aunt – and is execut-ing the clergy and stripping them of their wealth.

Luther agrees with the Pope about the desirability of a coun-cil but his idea of who needs persuading is the other way round. 'Christianity at large needs it,' he says, 'so that those parts that are yet to know error from truth, and have long existed in such a state, may see and understand this difference.'

Even papal envoys have a breaking point and eventually Ver-gerio can take no more. 'This is intolerable arrogance!' he explodes at length. 'It seems to me that your opinion is that the larger part of the good, wise and learned men of the world need only meet in a council ... and they will inevitably reach the same conclusions as you!' And Luther, no longer smiling, replies,

9

'I will come to the council, and I am willing to lose my head if I do not defend my opinions against the whole world. These things that proceed from my mouth are not my wrath, but the wrath of God!'

Later on, in his report to Rome, Vergerio compares Luther's eyes to 'those I have seen in some mad condemned man ... revealing fury and rage within. And indeed, the longer I reflect on what I have seen and heard in this monster and on the great power of his nefarious operations ... the more I am led to believe that he is possessed by some demon ... and it is to the infinite disgrace of these foolish princes and the others who govern these lands that they have not recognised what sort of person they have taken for their master and prophet!'

~

While Vergerio is breakfasting with Luther the Holy Roman Emperor is wending his way through his southern Italian possessions to Rome. The last time Charles V of the House of Hapsburg, King of all Spains, King of Germany, King of Italy, King of the Two Sicilies, Duke of Burgundy, Landgrave of Alsace, Count of Flanders and so on, privileged the Eternal City with his attention, back in 1527, his army sacked it and besieged Pope Clement until he paid a large ransom.

Eight years and a change of pontiff later, all is forgiven. Pope Paul has been enlarging his palace the better to share it with Charles and his men. The city is laying in food, fodder and all the wine the Tiber can carry while churches and a temple of Peace are demolished to give the Imperial army a clear run in; improvements that are financed in the usual way. 'If I had an ecu for each day of pardon the Pope wishes to sell,' writes François Rabelais, who is in town in his capacity as private doctor to the French ambassador, 'I would be richer than ...' And he gives the name of a long-dead treasurer of France who was obscenely wealthy.

Only this summer the Emperor added the North African slave mart of Tunis to his possessions, conquering it in person from the Sultan's high admiral or Captain Pasha, Hayreddin Barbarossa, and he naturally wishes to vaunt his success to his Italian subjects. But between Naples and Rome he gets bad news. Taking advantage of Charles's presence in the south of the peninsula, King Francis has sent in troops from the north, and his objective is the Duchy of Milan.

The rivalry goes back to 1519, when both men stood for election to the throne of the Holy Roman Empire that had fallen vacant on the death of Charles's grandfather Maximilian. Charles won that contest by bribing the electors fair and square, with Francis assuring him that the outcome would leave no bitterness, 'just as two suitors in love with the same lady do not fall into enmity'. But sincerity isn't Francis's strong suit, he breaks his word as easily as he breaks for tennis.

In 1525 the Most Christian King led a French army as far as Pavia, twenty miles from Milan, but he was defeated and captured by a Hapsburg force. He spent a year in one of Charles's prisons in Madrid before being released in exchange for the Dauphin and the Duke of Orleans and a pledge to surrender Burgundy. Francis never intended to give up Burgundy and eventually he purchased the freedom of his sons for two million gold ecus and a further promise to give up his Milanese claims – again, broken.

So it's a reflective emperor who enters Rome on 5 April, crosses the Tiber and is met by the Pope on the steps of St Peter's. Still he washes the feet of thirteen poor men on Maundy Thursday; still he kneels and rises in symmetry with the Pope on Easter Day. Only with the arrival in Rome of a French ambassador empowered to negotiate Milan's transfer to France does he act.

~

On 17 April the Emperor asks the French ambassador to follow him to the Pope's robing chamber. He and Paul lean against the Papal bed and the cardinals, the Venetian ambassador and other notables gather in a semicircle. Removing his bonnet and holding it before him as a gesture of respect, Charles declares that he has come to kiss the feet and hands of the Pope.

Charles is of medium height, with powerful arms and well-proportioned legs. His big green eyes are his best feature. His chin, which the rest of him follows at a respectful distance, is his worst.

Over the next hour and a half, speaking the Spanish he learned as a teenager after inheriting Castile and Aragon, Charles warms to his theme of French perfidy. Although he held Francis in his power after the Battle of Pavia, he explains, he magnanimously released him and married him to his sister Eleanor. And how did the Most Christian King respond? With violations, slanders and acts of war to which he responded only 'with great reluctance'.

The worst aspect of Francis's behaviour is his friendship with the Turk. The Most Christian King receives horses from his friends in Constantinople. He tips them off about Charles's troop movements and plots with them against the Emperor. In the opinion of no less an authority on scruple than Thomas Cromwell, nothing would deter Francis from bringing the Muslims into the heart of Christendom if by doing so he would gain Milan.

When the Turk launched his recent offensive in Hungary, threatening Germany, the Emperor asked Francis for help. The King replied that he would come with fifty thousand men on foot and three thousand cavalry – but to Italy, not Germany. So obsessed is Francis with capturing Milan, so indifferent to Germany's plight, that he told Charles that he would raise most of his footsoldiers from Germany and then complained at the discourtesy of the Emperor's response!

Even now it remains Charles's fondest wish to win over the King through honesty, unite against the Turk and restore the Church to health. But Francis's latest attempt to usurp Milan obliges the Emperor to set aside his well-known love of peace. And so – still leaning on the Papal bed, still speaking calmly – he announces that he will quit this city tomorrow and go north to invade France unless Francis 'wishes to meet me in person on a field of honour, either fully armed or in our shirts with only a sword or dagger, on land or sea, on a bridge or an island, in a designated space or in front of our armies, or wherever or however he wants'.

Three months later, Francis having responded to the Emperor's challenge with his usual levity, Charles invades Provence, loses eight thousand men and withdraws. The Pope continues to preach reconciliation. But unless the issues which lie between Francis and Charles are resolved by force or held in check by a stalemate, there can be no peace. The Pope urges a council. But the Christian princes can't agree on a venue for the council, let alone what it should discuss. And Venice, whose alliance with the Sultan has been fraying for some time, knows that she will bear the brunt of his arms if she joins the Emperor and the Pope in an anti-Turkish war.

~

In September 1537 a French flotilla led by the Baron de Saint-Blancard, master of the Provence Galleys, joins forces with the Turks off the Venetian island of Corfu. 'Joins forces' does not signify an equivalence of military might, the Turkish fleet numbering six hundred sail and the French flotilla twelve galleys, a frigate and a brig. The Turks greet their allies by firing their cannons and, in the words of Jean de Vega, a member of the baron's suite, 'never fell so fine a hail as the Turkish bullets that skimmed the sea.'

The next day Saint-Blancard is rowed ashore. Stepping onto Albanian soil he rides up a hill to an enormous tent where the Sultan's Grand Vizier, Ayas Pasha, awaits him. The Pasha greets the Baron by placing his hand on his chest, his mouth and finally his forehead.

'The aforementioned tent is called the Porte,' Vega reports, in reference to the Sublime Porte in Constantinople, and pains have indeed been taken to transfer the Ottoman seat of government in all its majesty from the Bosporus to the Ionian Sea.

From this hillside Porte a path leads to the Sultan's tent at the summit of a higher hill, more a town than a tent and encircled by a length of cloth painted to resemble a wall whose circumference exceeds that of the wall around Toulon. Along this wall stand three thousand Janissaries in close formation wearing robes of red, violet, deep blue or white, each man with his scimitar, small dagger and axe. The Janissaries are motionless except for those who fall softly from time to time, dead or dying from the plague, and are dragged away and replaced.

From his high point the Sultan looks onto twelve thousand tents that belong to his army and are spread over the hills in perfect order, and onto the sparkling sea below with his fleet in pleasing array. He looks across the strait to Corfu, which his brother-in-law Lutfi Pasha invaded a few days ago and which is oversmudged with smoke from a town that Lutfi's men are burning to the ground.

The Sultan receives Saint-Blancard in his tent seated on cushions of cloth of gold. He is wearing a white satin gown with a medium-sized turban over a bonnet of pleated crimson velvet. Pinned to the folds of the turban is a gold medallion or rosette with a cut ruby the size of a hazelnut and in his right ear is a pearl shaped like a pear and intricately wrought.

The Sultan has long delicate bones, a brown, oval face, forward cheekbones and a plausible chin (look on with envy, Charles, look on with envy!). His eyes are hazel, the same colour as Francis's, only deeper. He has an aquiline nose, long reddish moustaches, chin-hairs trimmed rather than shaved; and the famous neck, swan-like, hanging and sad.

During the interview the Frenchman regrets that he will be unable to join the Turks in their new war against Venice, which may not come as a surprise to the Sultan in view of the puny size of Saint-Blancard's fleet, lost in a forest of Ottoman masts.

After quitting the Sultan's presence, Saint-Blancard has a prospect of the Turks assaulting Corfu Town, watching the Turkish galleys running towards the citadel and firing at it while the Venetians return fire. The following day, 13 September, the French take on water at a place on Corfu that has fallen into

Turkish hands and hold Mass in a church that has received a visit from the invaders. The nave is full of corpses, the frescoes are covered in excrement and an image of the Virgin has been attacked by a Turk who, prising off a pilgrim's silver token that was fixed to it, was struck blind, since when no one has dared defile the place further.

~

One might think of Christendom as a house whose roof has been built by rival roofers using different materials laid to different pitches, the edges of each section rubbing against each other while other sections, inexplicably neglected, are open to the elements.

The house next door is the Muslim Caliphate which has a single roof built by a single craftsman according to a single plan: uniform, monotonous and effective. A roof that is easily extendable over any neighbouring house that may be annexed.

Under roofs live families, families composed of parents and their dependents, of people of the same faith or sect, of members of the same city, principality, kingdom or empire. Each family is a setting in which individuals interact with the group they belong to, each individual striving to avoid becoming a victim of circumstance.

Ottoman unity derives from a single idea, that of holy war leading to conquest, prosperity and divine favour. A desire for conquest animates the state and postpones the day, described by Ibn Khaldun of Tunis, when the tribe is fatally effeminised and subsides into decadence. That there is no such consensus under Christian roofs, no single idea, explains why, in the struggle between the two civilisations, the Christian family speaks with many voices and acts with many wills.

The irony of the unity gap is that while the Ottoman Caliphate excels at bonding the people, the army and the doctors of the law, the institution at its apex, the Sultan's family, is destined to self-destruct. No, 'destined' is too weak a word: it is required by law that the process of finding a sultan degenerate into a battle royal that only one candidate will survive.

That even a reign of piety and good sense must conclude in events abhorrent to God is a moral snare worthy of Niccolo Machiavelli, whose account of power has passed from hand to hand ever since he issued it in manuscript form a couple of decades ago. Not that Machiavelli admits God into his scheme, but deliberately excludes him, his treatise being an extended advocacy for any quality of character that enables one to take power and retain it, including cruelty and cunning.

The merit of Machiavelli is that he considers politics as it is, not as it should be. His flaw is that he ascribes to everyone motives as base as his own. With respect to his exemplar, Cesare Borgia, who, as son of Pope Alexander VI rose to become a powerful duke through the use of deception and callousness, his cynicism may be justified, but more often leaders long to be recognised as being not only just but also strong, faithful and powerful, and this may require the deception, not of others, but of oneself.

Sultan Suleyman belongs to this latter camp. If he survives his current phase of war and lives into old age, a question will pose itself, of how fair to fight and how far. A question that, while easy enough to answer for a godless bureaucrat stomping around his fields outside Florence, may be less so for someone whose person is sanctified, his conscience holy, his roof a crescent moon in a desert sky.

~

In the 1510s, when young Suleyman was apprenticing as Governor of the Aegean province of Manisa, his father Sultan Selim sent him a robe. The boy wanted to wear it but his mother Hafsa, knowing the sender, restrained him, and the poisoned robe killed the attendant who tried it on. In 1520, when Suleyman was informed that his father was dead and that he must come to Istanbul, he went in trepidation, fearing that it was a ruse to lure him away from safety and kill him.

In the course of his short reign Selim almost tripled the size of the Empire by invading Syria, Palestine, Egypt and Arabia.

He also defeated the Iranian Shah. When he wasn't fighting he spent much time in thought, when none of his pashas dared speak to him or offer him advice, and he governed quite alone and guided by these long periods of reflection. Suleyman, on the other hand, prefers to rule with the support and solidarity of those who enjoy his trust and affection.

The person who until recently enjoyed his trust and affection lies in an unmarked grave in a dervish convent behind the Imperial dockyard. At dawn the body was brought in its shroud from the Sultan's Privy Chamber down to the jetty at Seraglio Point. Then it was rowed the short distance across the Golden Horn. The month being Ramadan, the townsfolk had gone back to sleep after their pre-dawn meal and Ibrahim the Frank was in the ground before anyone knew what was happening. Since then a Judas tree has been planted nearby to give him shade. This must be a joke as it's the tree from which Judas Iscariot hanged himself after betraying Jesus.

Between 1523, when Suleyman named him Grand Vizier, and his death in 1536, Ibrahim had been called *makbul*, 'the favourite', which the poets have since, with typical economy of effort, changed to *maktul*, 'the killed one'.

> In the end, having been the favourite one forever,
> The favoured vizier became the killed one.
>
> Whosoever is unjust and pitiless
> Is undoubtedly worthy of death.
>
> That's the way destiny has always been,
> Everyone must reap what he has sown.

Not that Ibrahim was particularly unjust or pitiless. That's just the way the poem works. But the Muslims of Istanbul never took to the Sultan's convert chum, this wine-drinker who was born a citizen of the Venetian Republic and a follower of the Cross, and who was never happier than when discussing jewels with his friend the Venetian ambassador. And the first thing they did after his death was head for the Hippodrome and take revenge on the statues of three boozy, bawdy, fornicating Greek gods that he had brought back as mementoes from Buda and placed in front of his palace there.

He was the Empire's administrator and commander, the royal impresario who presented Suleyman to the world and spangled the walls of the New Palace with azure and gold.

Now he is erased from the record, his name hardly uttered, his resting place known only to a few, his palace, horses, gems and musical instruments and his fifteen hundred slaves absorbed into royal ownership. And each time Suleyman goes on campaign or sees Ibrahim's palace, each time he is reminded of their youth together – of the old woman, say, who approached them while they were hunting cranes near Yanbolu and offered them a pomegranate – his choice is to remember or push away.

It takes nerve to do what the Sultan did on the Ides of March 1536. To partake in aromatic dishes that have been devised to awaken the royal palate after the hours of fasting, to hear verses from the Quran recited sweetly and speak with one's closest friend before retiring on the warmest of terms, not together to the Sultan's bedchamber, those days of intimacy being long over, but to adjacent rooms – to do this while giving nothing away takes nerve.

Even now the room where Ibrahim slept and where he thrashed as the mutes pulled the bowstring around his neck is stained with blood. His blood is Suleyman's aide-memoire. Never again entrust the affairs of state to a slave who mistakes himself for the Sultan, never again let an official, no matter how high or trusted, into the Privy Chamber. The Sultan should not form emotional attachments to those he has raised to public office. He must not let those to whom he is attached influence affairs of state.

~

In Suleyman's library in the New Palace there is a Persian miniature, on dun paper, showing a lion and a bull on the verge of combat. The bull goes back on his haunches, his hide black and hard, his neck coiled, great his eyes, his ears pricked and his horns angled to meet the lion's leap, while the lion circles his prey with his eye of enjoyment, his little testicles swinging, the pads and calluses of his paw, his mane.

As a hunter there isn't much the Sultan can't do. He's as skilled at the backward arrow shot as he is at the forward. He is also proficient at falconry, which he practises on horseback, flighting the falcon from his forearm to rag a spotted deer, and while he is never alone, inasmuch as he is surrounded by pages and eunuchs and bodyguards who would lay down their lives for him unblinkingly, he is alone, for no man lives to hunt surrounded by payrolled sycophants.

He brought elephants on the Belgrade campaign of 1521, with their Indian keepers. Outside the fallen city, on the banks of the Danube, prisoners watched, awaiting their fate, as one of the elephants, its feet decked with anklets of gold, trampled their fellow captives to death, while above them Suleyman watched too, thinking his thoughts, seated on a throne pitched against a high hill.

Returning from that campaign, outside Philippopolis, he mounted a black Arabian stallion and slew a running mountain sheep with his sword, reaching down from his saddle and slicing into the sheep's fugitive body. He hunted, perhaps, with particular fury and desolation that day, having recently learned that his son Murat and his daughter Raziye were dead of the plague. A short while later, after his triumphal entry into Istanbul, another son, Mahmud, died from smallpox.

His sons. The alive and the dead. Would it be a surprise to learn that Suleyman, a man like any other, prefers not to think about the day when his surviving sons will kill each other till just one stands?

I I

For the past one hundred and fifty years infidel towns and villages newly occupied by the Ottoman army have paid a tax in boys. Severed from their families, these orphans find a new father in the Sultan, and since their destiny is tied to his, they become his devoted servants and are promoted to high office. For as long as the empire continues to expand, the Sultan's corps of slaves will not want for new entrants and the cycles of renewal will go on.

Jews and Armenians are exempt from the levy. So are only sons, orphans and the sons of village headmen, as is anyone who is conceited or full of himself. Tall boys are not taken because they are known to be stupid, nor are short boys because they are troublemakers. Boys who know Turkish or have been to Istanbul aren't eligible either.

Upon reaching the city the most promising are enrolled in preparatory school. They are circumcised, filled with Islam and taught Turkish, Arabic and Persian. They learn to paint, gild, engrave, pluck a zither and sing. They play a game in which they hit a ball with a stick, and another, on horseback, that involves throwing a blunt javelin at your opponent.

Every so often some of the boys are discharged into the populace or the army. Only the most beautiful and accomplished are admitted to the page school in the Third Court of the New

Palace, the feeder institution for the dedicated corps, known as chambers, that attend the Sultan.

The names of the chambers aren't always a reliable guide to their activities. Senior personnel in the Treasury Chamber include a man who is in charge of the Sultan's parrots and another who looks after his nightingales. Members of the Commissary collect rain- and rosewater during the month of April, which they offer to the Sultan in return for a reward. The Falconry Chamber does what it says on the tin.

And each chamber has its own complement of deaf mutes and dwarfs, the former to guard the Sultan when he is engaged in private conversation, keep his books, letters and secret writings in custody and carry out executions, and the latter for entertainment.

Whenever the pages speak they show each other great affection, calling each other 'my brother' or 'my soul'. But they seldom speak. The values prized in a page are intelligence, discipline and silence. The punishment for smiling during prayers is to be beaten five hundred times.

On holidays the pages are allowed to play games until dawn. They don satin and brocade caftans; they put on lace skullcaps, fine slippers, cummerbunds and sweet-smelling scents and the rules fall away.

From time to time during their progress from the palace school and through the various chambers, a selection of pages is made. The palace doorkeeper comes to the Sultan and tells him, 'Lord, the time has come for your slaves, who pray to God for your life, to come out of the palace.' The Sultan says, 'let it be so,' and the pages in question line up to kiss the hand of their lord, who is seated on a low seat placed on a most beautiful and grand carpet of silk and gold that has been spread in a small courtyard, with one hand over his dagger, and the other resting on his thigh, and they come one by one very cheerfully and reverently, and some kiss his hem, and others his foot, without saying a word. Once the Sultan has seen them all, he greets them and they, bowing deeply, indicate their gratitude before being sent away, often with a wife who has been released from harem service, and the Third Court becomes a memory.

With each disgorgement the pool of men from which the Sultan chooses his most trusted slaves gets smaller. Only the best are promoted from the Commissary to the Treasury and finally to the Sultan's Privy Chamber.

~

The Sultan isn't only the sultan. He is the Caliph of all Muslims and the custodian of the Holy Places of Mecca, Medina and Jerusalem. The Privy Chamber, besides being where he lives, also houses his most precious relics, including the robe worn by the Prophet Muhammad. The number of pages and officers attached to the Privy Chamber is never less than thirty-two and never more than forty. They live adjacent to the Sultan in their own rooms, protecting him and the artefacts that endue his sultanate with sanctity. They stand holding tapers at the corners of his bed while he sleeps. They mount a ceaseless watch over the robe of the Prophet, like the Zoroastrians guarding their eternal fires.

The head of the Privy Chamber is the most honoured, the best paid and the best dressed slave in the Empire. He stands next to the Sultan at ceremonies. He holds the Sultan's knife, which signifies the highest level of trust it is possible to attain, and presents him with titbits from costly plates during celebrations and festivals. He holds an Imperial seal, set in a ring, which he uses to seal the most precious objects in the royal apartments, such as the phials of sacred water into which a corner of the Prophet's robe has been dipped. Wherever the Sultan goes, whether it is to visit the mosque or invade Rhodes, the head of the Privy Chamber is with him.

In its cycles of domesticity the relationship between the Sultan and the head of the Privy Chamber resembles that between two members of the same family. But the slave's involvement in every aspect of his master's life is a passive one. The love that exists between two brothers, for instance, is made up of action and reaction, parry and counter-parry, evidence for human autonomy that a slave may not exhibit. In order to embody the devotion that is expected of him, the head of the Privy Chamber must give up the instruments of his autonomy. He must stand outside conventional identity, beyond the poles of gender and desire.

~

Typically the child is restrained on a seat; the penis and scrotum are tied with a cord which is pulled taut, and the penis, scrotum and testes are removed with a single stroke of the razor. Boiling oil is applied to stop the bleeding and the wound is dressed with an extract of wax and tallow. A lead nail may be introduced into the urethra to stop it contracting.

The survivors are sold for a high price and the royal physicians, having inspected the specimen on arrival to ensure that both penis and testes have been removed, re-examine him periodically to confirm that nothing is amiss. Possible problems include strictures that make it impossible for him to empty his bladder, which is overcome by using a silver quill as a catheter. In the case of the opposite problem it is necessary to stop the opening with a removable plug to prevent undignified flooding.

Cyrus the Great of Persia gave little credence to the view that eunuchs are weaklings, observing that vicious horses, when castrated, stop biting and prancing but are none the less fit for service in war, while dogs that undergo the same procedure stop running away from their masters but remain useful for hunting. Both in combat and the chase castrated men show that they preserve a spirit of rivalry; and no one ever performed greater acts of loyalty than eunuchs. Cyrus selected eunuchs for every post of personal service to him, from the doorkeeper up.

Aristotle was concerned with externalities. He noted that if you emasculate a cockerel by burning him twice or thrice at the rump with hot irons, if the bird is fully grown, his crest will

become sallow, he will cease to crow and he will show no interest in sexual activity, while if you castrate him when he is young
none of these male attributes will come to him. The same is true
of men. If you mutilate them in boyhood the later-growing hair
never grows and the voice remains high-pitched, but if they are
mutilated in early manhood the later growth of hair is shed
except for the growth on the groin, which diminishes without
falling entirely. In general, mutilated animals grow to a greater
length than unmutilated ones and, if operated upon when they
are young, they become bigger and better-looking than their
unmutilated fellows. You never see a bald eunuch though you
often see a tall one.

~

Hadim Suleyman should not be confused with Sultan Suleyman. He was enslaved and sold in Hungary in the 1460s and
rose to become head of the Privy Chamber under Sultan Selim.
The moniker Hadim, or 'servant', is a way of saying that someone is a palace eunuch but not in so many words.

Shortly after Sultan Suleyman came to the throne he replaced
Hadim Suleyman with Ibrahim the Frank, which caused a scan-
dal because Ibrahim wasn't a eunuch and hadn't risen through
the chamber system, but the infatuated Sultan did it anyway.
Approaching sixty years of age, the Hadim could have retired in
luxury and spent the rest of his days counting his slaves and
horses. But having things is an overrated pleasure if you've no
one to share them with, and counting them is a joke if you
know that the moment you die they will go to the Sultan and it
will be as if you never existed.

So when the Hadim left the Privy Chamber he chose an active
life, following in the steps of distinguished eunuchs like Gany-
medes, tutor to Cleopatra's half-sister Arsinoe, who became
Caesar's worthy adversary; or like Zheng He of China, who
rose from being a household eunuch to ruling the waves from
Java to Africa. Geldings, so to speak, with balls.

The Hadim's first palace job was in the Second Court, as

chief treasurer. After that he was sent to Syria as Governor and then to the Hungarian frontier with instructions to defend the Sultan's lands and run spies behind enemy lines. And so informative were his reports back to Istanbul, one would be forgiven for assuming that he had spent a lifetime scoping bastions and mapping rivers, not scratching the Sultan's back.

In 1525 Suleyman sent him to Egypt as Governor. While the Hadim was in Cairo he formed an attachment to a people of Yemen, far to the south at the mouth of the Red Sea. From this people, whose ancestors were called Ad, tall of stature and followers of the Prophet Hud, he took one thousand manly youngsters of outstanding beauty and stoutness of heart, dressed them in fine clothes and gave each one a golden belt and dagger. Not that the Hadim's taste in slaves was solely aesthetic. They showed the way his lance was pointing.

~

Cairo is separated from the Gulf of Suez by eighty miles of desert. The Gulf of Suez is connected to the Red Sea which descends to the Gate of Lamentation, which is a strait rather than a gate and so called because it has widowed and orphaned many. If you sail east from here, along the coasts of Yemen and Oman and across the Arabian Sea, you come to Gujarat, hub of the external trade of India. It is a matter of regret that this trade belongs to Portugal, whose colonies and clients constitute a huge maritime empire, an equatorial Venice whose galleys enter the Red Sea and sink Ottoman ships at will.

As is laid out in painful detail in the *Book of the Sea*, a recent Turkish guide to the oceans, it was Vasco da Gama who rounded the Cape of Good Hope and reached India, and Columbus who discovered the New World, while the Sultan also has among his possessions a Portuguese chart showing Magellan's circumnavigation of the globe. That the Ottomans possess so secret a chart indicates that their spies have penetrated the House of India, those rooms in Lisbon's Ribeira Palace from where the King of Portugal's men organise his convoys, enforce his spice monopoly and issue orders to his viceroy in Goa, the Empire's forward base. But no feat of espionage can hide the fact that the Ottomans have no eastern empire and no House of India of their own.

In 1535 Bahadur Shah, King of Gujarat, asked the Portuguese for help against his Mughal foes to the north, but having let the infidels into Diu, his most valuable port, he found them unwilling to leave. So the King dispatched his treasure and harem to Mecca, thus placing them under Ottoman protection. And he asked the Sultan, defender of Muslims everywhere, to expel the Portuguese.

Two years later the Portuguese Viceroy dropped anchor at Diu and invited Bahadur onto his flagship. Feigning illness the Viceroy regretted that he could not rise to greet his guest, but if he would only wait, he would receive presents. Uneasy, Bahadur decided to return to his barge. Hit by a Portuguese spear he fell into the water and diving like a pearl, as the saying goes, his rising place was paradise. In Istanbul the Sultan sorrowfully exercised his right to the expired pilgrim's effects, receiving two hundred and fifty chests containing one and a quarter million measures of gold.

For years the two Suleymans have contemplated the conquest of India. Now they have their chance, Bahadur's murder supplying the pretext, his treasure the means.

~

In the days of the pharaohs Suez was a city of cisterns. During the annual Nile flood, water entered the canal that linked the two and the cisterns were replenished, enough to last till the following year. But less wise rulers neglected the canal and it was buried under sand. Nowadays the only refreshment at Suez is brackish water brought in from distant wells.

One of the Hadim's projects was to revive the canal, which would have solved the water problem and allowed spice ships from India access to the Mediterranean via the Nile. But eighty miles is eighty miles, the sand didn't cooperate and the plan was shelved. So the Hadim must build his armada in the desert rather than in a city full of water and shade.

Over the winter of 1537 slaves and sailors in Suez turn pine logs into hulls, bitumen into caulkage and hemp into rigging, all of which is assembled into galleys, galliots, flat-bottomed mahones and foists, which are like galleys in that they are propelled by both sails and oars, only smaller. Seventy-six vessels in all, each assembled using supply chains that extend the length and breadth of the Empire. Only the flax for sails and flour for ship's biscuit are sourced locally.

Hadim Suleyman's force consists of Turks, Circassians and Africans, free men and slaves. Venice's contribution takes the form of sailors trapped by the recent outbreak of war between the Sultan and the Serenissima. Venetian slaves are among the mutineers who on a prearranged signal make a beeline for the hills behind Suez where they are intercepted by the Turkish cavalry and returned to the oar bench naked and in chains.

~

In June the Hadim reaches Suez. He would disappoint Aristotle, being neither taller nor better-looking than his unmutilated fellows. On the contrary, he is so fat that he cannot move under his own power but needs the help of four men whenever he wishes to resile from a sitting position. Light-skinned, as one might expect from someone of his Hungarian ancestry, beardless and wizened, he bears some slight resemblance to a bleached date.

But the Hadim is not sweet to taste and there are many who attest to his cruelty. It's hard to imagine him calling anyone 'my soul', with the exception of his Yemeni slaves.

The Hadim is the only member of Sultan Selim's old guard who was retained by Suleyman. He was the first Governor of Egypt to remit the tax revenue, referred to reverentially as the Egyptian Treasure, that contributes so handsomely to the Imperial exchequer. In 1531 he safely brought that year's Egyptian Treasure, all eight hundred thousand ducats of it, in person to the Grand Vizier.

He was at Rhodes when Suleyman took the island from the Knights Hospitaller in 1522. He was at Baghdad for the conquest of that city in '34. He held the knife of the present Sultan's father.

Never underestimate the importance of trust.

~

From Suez to its mouth the Red Sea extends twelve hundred miles in length and two hundred miles in width. For its whole length it is full of banks, shoals and shelves. To follow the right course it is necessary to station an experienced pilot on the prow calling left or right according to circumstance.

On the first night after setting sail the fleet drops anchor at the place where Moses divided the sea with his rod and Pharaoh and his army were drowned. The next stop is the jumping off point for Mount Sinai, where Saint Catherine rests. On 11 July the fleet reaches Jeddah, burial place of Eve, a stage and a half from Mecca. Wherever you are on the Judaeo-Islamic spectrum the Red Sea has something for you.

From the island of Kamaran Hadim Suleyman sends messengers to the lord of Zabid, a city of Yemen, telling him to bring tribute, but although the foist returns with gifts of wrought swords and daggers embedded with turquoise and rubies, of the lord himself there is no sign. On sails the armada, past islands frequented by pearl divers, along coasts whose trees give a resin that Christians burn in their churches, and safely through the Gate of Lamentation, into the Gulf of Aden and on to the port city of the same name.

In 1513 the Portuguese sent twenty ships to take Aden but their landing parties were repulsed, the city's natural defences being augmented by bastions that reach for the sky. Even if a large expeditionary force were successfully landed at Aden, subduing the place might take weeks.

The huge Turkish armada that drops anchor on 3 August generates a different awe. The fore-and-aft sails in a chequerboard pattern of green and purple, the deck awnings covered in flags and the long banners streaming so far down from the mastheads that the ends brush the surface of the water all say: don't fuck with me. And Amir bin Daoud, the local prince, is prompt to send four persons of quality aboard Hadim Suleyman's ship to pay their respects, armed with refreshments, eyes and ears. Not that they call him Hadim, at least not to his face, but Suleyman Pasha, in recognition of his recent promotion.

The Hadim talks privately with the delegation before giving each member two jackets of figured velvet and sending them ashore with letters of safe conduct for the Amir, indicating that he may come aboard freely, fearing nothing. The Amir replies that he will not come but that he will give the Turks everything they want. This unsatisfactory answer vexes the Hadim for the rest of that day and the whole of the next.

On 5 August he orders some Janissaries ashore to fetch the Amir and this time he does come aboard, along with his nobles, and the Hadim puts him at his ease by giving him two jackets as well as garments for each lord, and objects in gold, and the mood is conviviality itself. Then the Hadim's men seize the Amir and hang him from the mast and again some Janissaries come ashore, this time to occupy the city, and after taking on water the armada sails on.

~

Diu is an island with a town at one end and a fort at the other and a channel separating it from the mainland. The fort guards the entrance to the harbour and is surrounded by a wall with towers at regular intervals.

The Hadim's local ally is Hoja Safar, a renegade of Italian origin who served Bahadur Shah and almost managed to save him from the Portuguese spears. A man of resource, in other words, for which quality Bahadur Shah awarded him Diu – provided he could take it from the Portuguese. And by the time the Hadim drops anchor within three miles of the island, on 4 September, Hoja Safar is halfway to achieving that objective, having chased the infidels from Diu town and into the fort.

Hoja Safar comes aboard and explains that he wants enough artillery to knock down the walls. What he doesn't want is for the Hadim's eight thousand Janissaries to land and change facts on the ground. Hoja has in mind an absentee overlord to protect Muslim trade by sea and smilingly waft pilgrims to Mecca, not a new colonial power.

But this is to misunderstand the Turks and their mission. It was a source of frustration to Sultan Selim that the Spanish beat him to the New World and that the Portuguese beat him to the East, and it remains so to his son.

The Janissary Corps' recent battle honours include Chaldiran, in 1514, which smashed the power of Iran, and Mohacs, twelve years later, when they annihilated the army of King Louis of Hungary and turned much of his kingdom into an Ottoman tributary. Facts on the ground are what the Janissaries do.

Then there are the Hadim's personal circumstances to consider. He turned down retirement in favour of a life of trial. He built the biggest armada to ply these waters since Zheng He's dragon ships a century ago. He hasn't gone to all this trouble simply to supply ordnance to some hard-pressed natives.

While the Hadim regales Hoja Safar with gifts and the two men exchange pleasantries the town of Diu is being sacked and every kind of indignity is visited on its inhabitants, including houses stripped of their contents and stables of their horses, and no, these outrages aren't committed by the Portuguese but by the same Janissaries who have come ashore and are recognisable by their rich crimson satins and white felt caps edged with gold, and who, after terrorising their allies, advance to the fort to terrorise their foes.

~

There is a redoubt on the channel's mainland shore, defended by a Portuguese force led by Francisco Pacheco. After a bombardment lasting twenty days Pacheco surrenders and the Turks enter and run up a large red flag bearing the Sultan's crescent. In a letter dictated by the Pasha, Pacheco urges the commander of the Portuguese forces in the fort across the channel, Antonio da Silveira, to surrender to the Pasha whom he praises for being wise and just. In his reply Silveira marvels that so wise and just a Pasha can be so full of lies. And he sends a message to the Pasha that 'we intend to die on the smallest stone of this fort.'

On 4 October the Ottoman cannons and mortars open fire with copper balls, chains and stones wrapped in oiled leather and sheepskins. The defenders soon work out that the best material for filling breaches is recycled masonry, so while the Turks are busy destroying the walls the Portuguese demolish their own houses and use the stone to plug the gaps. And although the attackers boast one hundred and thirty artillery pieces, including nine monster guns, and ten thousand fighting men to Silveira's six hundred soldiers and eleven hundred civilians, the fort holds out because one side has a leader and the other a recluse.

'Because of his efforts,' a comrade writes of Antonio da Silveira, 'the most fearful, laying eyes on him, not only lost their fear but found courage . . . [H]e would help everyone, and he would tend to every wounded and sick person . . . [T]he more the fear and travails grew, the more his diligence and compassion were aroused.'

Hadim Suleyman, by contrast, leads from behind, or rather from his ship, not that he cares to disclose which ship, having lowered his colours to avoid assassination, and when he orders a ring of cables and other impenetrable materials to be set up on his poop, sufficient to repel cannon-shot, it is clear that this man who is cavalier with the lives of others is reluctant to put himself in harm's way.

Some weeks into the siege the Turks' numerical superiority begins to tell, but as the Portuguese men fall the women rise. Donna Isabel de Vega, a woman of singular virtue and beauty, summons every member of her sex and they fetch water for the defenders and stones to mend breaches. Anne Fenandez is a mother to all, her cloths and bandages on every wound, and with her staff and candle she patrols the sentry posts at night, explaining how much effort is required to defend life and honour. She suffers the death of her own son with such stoicism that no soldier dares retreat from the heat of battle for fear of her disapproval.

In the early hours of 30 October the Turks plant scaling ladders while a second party mounts the breach on the land side. Amid savage fighting, first Turkish then Portuguese colours are hoisted above what used to be walls and are now smouldering ribbons of rubble, ash and flesh. Anne Fenandez is spotted holding aloft the image of the Redeemer while another defender runs out carrying a barrel of powder and cries 'clear the way, for here I carry my own and many a man's death!' He and a dozen Turks are tossed skywards.

For four hours the battle rages until the defenders are so scorched that a brother flees from his brother, thinking him a ghost. By the time the Turks withdraw a mere forty defenders are able to bear arms and they are out of powder. The walls are shattered and further resistance is impossible. But behind his ring of cables the Hadim doesn't know how close he is to victory.

And his local ally Hoja Safar has had enough, enough of the Turkish arrogance and the uneasy sense that he is being taken for a fool. At every opportunity he reminds Hadim Suleyman that a Portuguese relief force is on its way from Goa and on 2 November the Hadim's nerve fails and he sets sail for home.

While the Turkish fleet is returning across the Arabian Sea, the Hadim sends for a member of his entourage, a person of note, and without giving a reason orders his head to be cut off. He perhaps anticipated that this person would accuse him of negligence or cowardice in the Sultan's hearing. After stopping at Aden and reinforcing the garrison there he continues to the Red Sea where he pauses to subdue Zabid and execute its insolent lord. The hundred and forty-six Portuguese prisoners he has on board are a waste of space so they are decapitated and their noses and ears are sent to the Sultan. The head of

Francisco Pacheco, who surrendered his redoubt early in the siege, is flayed and the skin is salted and filled with straw.

Putting into Jeddah the Hadim accomplishes the pilgrimage to Mecca, after which he goes to Istanbul where he is given a place on the Imperial Council as the vanquisher of Yemen.

India can wait.

III

How the Turks boast of the ease with which they pick and choose their tactical alliances among the Christians! And how the Christians envy Sultan Suleyman his unity of command, his lack of Lutherans, his resources without limit! There is no question of international politics that does not involve him. There is nothing he involves himself in that is not a question of international politics. He looks north, south, east and west, he looks to the waves as well as the land. He can cover the earth with troops and his people barely notice. And while committing men to several theatres at the same time inevitably places a strain on supply and personnel, it's a good kind of strain, the kind associated with vitality and health.

Among the Sultan's peers only the Emperor is his equal as a warrior prince, Francis being a part-timer, and Henry . . . well, Henry is too busy getting rid of his wives to do much fighting. And yet Suleyman, who since coming to the throne has invaded Belgrade, Rhodes, much of Hungary, Baghdad and too many Mediterranean, or White Sea, ports and pinpricks to name, has the unlikely reputation among his people of lacking the belly for a fight.

This judgement can only stem from a widespread tendency to compare him to his father, who took bellicosity to unhealthy extremes. Next to his grandfather Bayezid, who restricted himself to small wars, Suleyman's record as an aggressor cannot be faulted. As for the market-place bores who complain about his retreat from Vienna in the autumn of 1529, they don't know the Austrian winters.

Whenever the Sultan writes to his fellow monarchs, he opens with the words, 'I am the great lord and conqueror of the whole world.' Charles might have something to say about that. The portrait of the Emperor that Parmigianino painted to mark his coronation in 1530 shows an infant Hercules offering him a globe.

Charles's dominions grew to their current discontinuous sprawl through marriage alliances. In the name of administrative coherence the Emperor has handed Austria and Bohemia to his brother Ferdinand and the Netherlands to his sister Maria. But it doesn't help that as king of both Spain and Germany he must host France in his midriff.

Suleyman's empire, by contrast, was acquired by painstaking conquest over many centuries, one territory after another. Istanbul is its epicentre, whose power radiates strongest in an inner band of directly administered provinces, weakens in an outer band of tributaries, then fades.

Ever since his accession Suleyman has probed to see where his fading points are, with provisional findings that include Austria, the Atlantic and now India. And while it would be nice to have Vienna, Gujarat and the Americas, he can live without them. What he cannot live without is the basin by the epicentre: his lake, his highway, his Achilles heel.

~

If you are invited by Paolo Giovio, bishop, retired Papal doctor and well-connected observer of events, to visit and see the portraits he has hung in his new villa on Lake Como, be sure to stop before Bronzino's depiction of Andrea Doria as Neptune. In the picture Doria is naked except for a length of sailcloth, and he stands on the deck of his ship before an oppressive Mediterranean sky, lit up by a flash of distant lightning and showing off rippling muscles, a proud belly and a thick, strong oar.

In July just before dawn a flotilla commanded by Doria

surrounded twelve Turkish galleys near the island of Paxos. Doria directed his men from the tabernacle of his ship, as if addressing the Turks: is this all you've got? When his ships returned to the Hapsburg port of Messina they were towing all twelve enemy vessels.

Apart from being god of the sea, Doria is the ruler of Genoa and is the Emperor's high admiral. He and Barbarossa are the Mediterranean's celebrity sailors, on opposite sides in the great struggle between Charles and Suleyman for world domination, and while Doria made his reputation as a scourge of pirates, Barbarossa is the biggest pirate around. So it's puzzling, to say the least, that these septuagenarian siblings of the sea, who have spent much of their lives attacking each other's interests, possessions and allies, have yet to meet squarely in battle.

There's nothing sinister about enemies talking, particularly in a neighbourhood as chatty as the Mediterranean, swapping slaves, ransoming nobles and exchanging cannonballs one moment and storm warnings the next. But you don't need to be Machiavelli to recognise that a defeated Doria would diminish Hayreddin's importance in the Sultan's eyes while Barbarossa's destruction would make Doria less vital to the Emperor.

It didn't go unnoticed that Barbarossa gave Doria the slip a little too easily after fleeing Tunis in 1535 and that the Captain Pasha exempts the Genoese island of Chios from his policy of tormenting any place that doesn't belong to the Sultan. A policy that may be connected to the tears of Chios, also known as mastic, which drips from trees on the island and is prized by the dessert-makers of the New Palace, and also to Barbarossa's reliance on Genoese middlemen to supply the Cornish tin that goes into his best bronze cannons. Who can tell what kind of sniffing and licking takes place between the old dogs amid the practised snarling and snapping?

For Doria the real foe isn't Turkey. It's Venice. Members of the Doria family have been leading Genoese fleets into battle against the Serenissima ever since Lamba Doria destroyed the Venetian fleet at Curzola in 1298.

During the Turkish assault on Corfu last autumn the Venetians sent Doria a plea for help. And Doria replied that nothing would please him more, but his ships were in poor condition and lacking soldiers and it would not be an honourable course of action, far less a prudent one, to risk the Emperor's prestige on a lost cause, but if the Venetians were of a mind to fight Suleyman with joint arms next year, no power on earth would prevent him, Doria, from coming to their aid.

In the event, and without Doria's intervention, the Turkish invasion was rebuffed and Christendom was treated to a rare sighting of the Sultan withdrawing an expeditionary force commanded by Lutfi Pasha, his own brother-in-law, job unfinished.

And next year is now. 1538. Time for Doria to lift his sailcloth.

~

You won't find Hayreddin posing as Neptune or boasting of his ancestors but the mothers of the White Sea have him to thank for their docile children. 'Hush or Barbarossa will come!' And the brat falls silent.

Taking note of his North African empire and his hatred of the Spanish, in 1534 Suleyman brought him in and gave him a budget. Not that the Captain Pasha is a particular drain on Ottoman resources. On the contrary, he and his associates, graduates cum laude of his Sorbonne of piracy and mayhem, help finance their activities by enslaving Christians and seizing their goods.

The Captain Pasha's shipmate Murat has been chronicling his skills as a chaos-maker. 'He went to the island of Crete,' opens Murat's account of the current campaign, 'and took five castles and that island being a big island he waged war and sailed seven hundred miles around the island and approaching from one side captured and destroyed and burned two more castles and seized more than fifteen thousand captives, young and old, girls and boys, and seized a large galley and that too was sent to Istanbul . . .'

In summer he is a terrorist, in winter a civil servant. In foul weather he does battle with supply and recruitment, tramping the Istanbul dockyard and glaring at the carpenters and caulkers from under his famous overhanging canopy of brows and lashes.

~

Affronted by the Sultan's attack on Corfu and made bold by the island's successful defence, in February 1538 Venice joins a Holy League against the Turks. Andrea Doria is to direct the combined fleet, Corfu is the rendezvous and the objective is the Ottoman-held fortress of Prevesa, situated at the entrance to the Ambracian Gulf in the Ionian Sea.

The Venetian squadron at Corfu with its ninety-one galleys is commanded by Vincenzo Capello. In June thirty-six galleys belonging to the Pope also arrive. Of the commander-in-chief, however, there is no sign. The weeks pass and the Papal force mounts a speculative assault on Prevesa which the Turks easily repulse. Only in the first week of September does Doria finally reach Corfu and the combined force set sail. Several weeks of good weather have been lost.

The Ambracian Gulf is a well-protected inland sea. It is reached through a channel between Prevesa, on the northern side of the entrance, and the site of ancient Actium on the southern side. Turkish guns overlook from both sides. And the channel itself is both narrow and shallow, such that big ships can only pass through in single file. By mid September, when the League's fleet arrives at the mouth of the Gulf, Barbarossa is inside.

Setting out for Crete in June he had just forty ships. Ninety had to be left on the stocks because they weren't ready. Even now he has thirty-seven fewer vessels than Doria and many of these are small galliots that would be no match for the Christian galleys in a formal engagement. He has at most five thousand soldiers to the enemy's twenty thousand so a land battle wouldn't suit him either.

A pragmatist – a Doria – would argue that Barbarossa should sit tight in his hospitable gulf, enjoy the fruits of the surrounding countryside and wait for the Christians to exhaust their provisions while being tossed in autumn seas. Then watch them go away.

But Sultan Suleyman doesn't like infirmity of purpose. And Hayreddin isn't that kind of admiral. So he sends fifty ships through the strait and into the open sea to gauge Christian intentions.

Vincenzo Capello is close at hand when the Turkish ships emerge and he pounces with his galleys. The Turks race back towards the channel while their pursuers' heavy guns pour cannonballs into their sterns. All the while Capello spurs his men with promises of immortal glory and rich spoils.

Now Doria has an opportunity to intercept the fleeing Turks before they reach the safety of the channel. Time for the Holy League to justify its existence. But to Capello's disbelief and fury Doria hangs back from the fray. Not only that; he signals to the Venetians to abandon their pursuit on pain of severe punishment!

When the Christian commanders convene off the nearby island of Santa Maura, Doria is at pains to sound like a tactician, not a traitor. 'We have dislodged the enemy,' he says, 'but . . . if we give battle, on these few hours will rest not only this armada but . . . the well-being of Christendom. For if this force is lost, what resources will remain with which to construct another?' Capello replies coldly that he has orders from his Senate to fight the Turkish fleet and he will do so. 'So be it,' Doria concedes, 'and let God favour our boldness.'

By now Barbarossa and his ships are out of the Gulf and in open waters. Barbarossa's column is in the middle, those of his pupils Salih and Turgut on either side. And these boys can sail. When Hayreddin's centre turns, his wheeling flanks spread so perfectly that the manoeuvre resembles an eagle opening its wings.

As Murat reports, 'when the Christian fleet saw the fleet of the righteous ones they came to meet them ... they had the wind at their backs, and if that wind came quickly the [Turkish] galliots would be destroyed by the heavy [Christian] galleys. At this prospect the Muslims' hearts filled with fear. Hayreddin Pasha wrote ... two verses from the Quran and when he dropped them from either side of his ship the wind died and those onrushing galleys were becalmed ... the sea became a millpond such that one might think that the wind had never blown, or that the sea had fallen asleep.'

God helps the deserving. By the following morning, 28 September, the Christians are strung out halfway to Santa Maura, their galleys needing to be towed if they are to move at all. On a windless sea the advantage lies with Barbarossa's lighter vessels. Plying his oars he approaches the Christian ships cautiously, keeping close to the shore so that if necessary he can beach his galleys from the stern with their guns bearing out to sea. But the Christians are in disarray. Hoisting red banners, to the sound of cymbals, drums and trumpets, the Turks surround the allied ships and open fire.

The battle lasts three hours during which Barbarossa sends one ship to the bottom with three hundred Spanish soldiers aboard and takes a Papal galley without resistance. Two Venetian ships catch fire and sink with all hands except for those who throw themselves into the burning waters screaming the name of their patron saint, San Gennaro, and are preyed upon by Hayreddin's archers. The only cause for cheer among the Venetians is the resistance of their flagship, the *Galeone di Venezia*, which, destitute of mast, bridge and railings, nonetheless causes considerable damage to her assailants. When they are not swinging their scimitars Barbarossa's men hang from ropes down to the waterline, patching holes.

At dusk Doria gives the order to return to Corfu under a freshening wind. The Turks give pursuit until nine o'clock when the Christian ships become silhouettes before disappearing into the darkness. 'See how Andrea Doria extinguishes all the lanterns so it cannot be seen where he flees,' Hayreddin scoffs.

Then there is a storm and the Turks are driven up against the Albanian coast.

When the Venetians get home they speak with new respect of Barbarossa. And it is reckoned that he satisfied every expectation a ruler can have of a prudent and valiant captain, and that his armada always remained well ordered, well disposed for battle and able to take any course.

The Venetians also say that the night before the battle two galliots were seen coming away from the Turkish forces at Prevesa, one of which went to Palermo, a town belonging to the Emperor, while the other came alongside Doria's galley before returning to Barbarossa.

Whatever the truth of these rumours, for some days after the battle Doria is not seen in public and for a long time after that whenever the subject of Prevesa is raised in his presence he appears barely able to hold back his tears in recognition of his failure and that of the Holy League, humiliated at sea and exposed for the fantasy it undoubtedly is.

IV

In the old days Suleyman would visit the palace of Alvise Gritti and sit in the unbeliever's garden until three in the morning amiably declining his offer of a gem-encrusted saddle worth one hundred thousand ducats. Alvise was the bastard son of the Doge of Venice whom the young Sultan allowed to dominate the Empire's external trade and become rich. And who all the while, as we now know, was working part-time for his fellow Christians and full-time for himself.

By the summer of 1534 Alvise had forfeited his position of trust at the Porte. When he marched northwards that June, he intended to go over to Ferdinand, Archduke of Austria and Bohemia, the Emperor's kid brother. For all his disquiet at the Venetian's treachery, however, when Gritti was besieged and beheaded by rebels whilst travelling northwards through Transylvania, Suleyman was far from pleased. The punishment of crimes is the monopoly of the Sultan and the insult to his royal prestige was as great, if not as terminal, as the injury to Gritti himself.

The treasure that Gritti had been dragging along with him, all one and a quarter million ducats of it, was trousered by his assassins. Ferdinand took advantage of the resulting weakening of the Sultan's authority to form a pact with Hungary's King Janos, who is supposed to be an Ottoman vassal.

Wrongs that need righting.

At daybreak on 6 July 1538, as the fleet of the Holy League assembles at Corfu, the people of Istanbul who have been waiting patiently overnight are rewarded with a view of the Sultan going to war.

At the head of the parade march the water carriers with their full skins, then two thousand mules, nine hundred horses and five thousand camels laden with supplies and munitions. Then come the armourers, one thousand in total, five hundred sappers, eight hundred bombardiers, four hundred soldiers of the imperial train with their commanders, adjutants and scribes, and gun carriages drawn by water buffalo, as valuable as they are bad-tempered. Next the cavalry divisions, two thousand to each wing, and twelve thousand Janissaries followed by mercenaries, each man equipped with his bow, scimitar, lance and mace.

The Sultan's personal escort is led by men holding seven gold-striped banners and is followed by one hundred trumpeters, their instruments slung around their necks on gold chains, one hundred kettledrummers and four hundred white-plumed archers, their royal master riding in their midst as if shaded by their plumes. And the streets are so full of religious students and dervishes offering prayers for his safe return that it is past midday before he exits the city in a westerly direction.

When the army reaches Edirne it is supplemented by those of Rumelia, corresponding to the Empire's Balkan possessions south of the Danube, and of Anatolia, or Asia Minor. Also at Edirne, in his palace on the banks of the Tundzha, the Sultan receives Mani, son of the ruler of Basra, who has come all this way to hand over the keys to the city. And thus he experiences the pleasant sensation, afforded to relatively few of us, of acquiring a distant place of strategic value without really trying.

The Balkan Peninsula is a thick trunk with many ridges and furrows into Europe. In 1532 the Sultan continued westwards from Edirne before swinging north towards Belgrade and the battlefields of Austria. Last year he went along the old Via Egnatia as far as the Adriatic. This time he takes a sharp northward turn at Edirne keeping the Black Sea to his right. Coming through the Danubian plain the army picks up more horsemen from the Sultan's fief-holders.

It isn't often that an Ottoman army perishes from hunger or undersupply. Centuries of experience have taught the planners how much food and fodder to take. If additional supplies are needed the army treasurers pay promptly and the people whose lands they pass through willingly bring them whatever is necessary as if to a common market. If boats are required for river crossings, this too is anticipated and couriers ride ahead to pass on instructions to the local lord.

On the Danube's northern bank Suleyman is greeted by his army which has crossed before him. Motionless on their chargers, with spears, lances and halberds erect to the sky, the armies of Rumelia and Anatolia resemble a huge bed of reeds. Particularly striking are the Janissary commanders with their golden girdles and the divisions of horse clothed from head to foot in thick mail.

Irregulars from Bilecik have been serving the Ottoman dynasty ever since their chief Mihal the Beardless helped the Sultan's ancestor Orhan conquer north-western Anatolia two centuries ago. They dress irregularly, in bear and tiger furs, with eagle wings and wolfskin caps. Their maces, long chains and swords glint, their spurs spin menacingly.

After passing through the corridor formed by his men Suleyman enters his tent and is informed that Petru Rares, Voivode of Moldavia and his rebellious tributary on Transylvania's eastern border, is playing for time.

~

Four summers ago, when Alvise Gritti was under siege and fighting for his life, Petru promised to send help only for his relief force to join the besiegers and come away with Alvise's head, possibly his two sons – not that they lived to tell the tale – and his treasure. Since then Petru has been making nice with Ferdinand. Not conduct that can remain unpunished.

It is three hundred and fifty miles from the Danube to Petru's capital of Suceava and there are more rivers in between. On 6 September the Ottoman army reaches the Prut which is more a morass than a river, and of all the Sultan's engineers the only one capable of building a bridge that doesn't sink is a young Janissary called Sinan. The Turks press on into the forests of southern Moldavia where the Sultan rests his head in Petru's hunting lodge but of Petru himself there is no sign.

Before setting out from Istanbul Suleyman sent a summons to Sahip Giray, Khan of the Crimean Tatars. The Tatars pack horsepower, each man bringing with him three or four spare mounts, and distance is no object; they last popped up in the Austrian campaign of '32. The conjunction of the two forces takes place outside the central Moldavian town of Iasi where the Tatar princelings file into the royal tent in their split-brim hats to kiss the Sultan's hand. Then the combined army burns Iasi to the ground.

Helpless before a host of this size, Petru flees into the Carpathian Mountains. The Sultan occupies Suceava and instals Petru's grandson. He instructs a sharp-nosed steward called Hussein to find Alvise Gritti's treasure and sure enough Hussein unearths a trove of horns, rapiers, pitchers, goblets, swords, jewels, embroidered shirts, books with gold and silver covers, Bibles, silks and money.

On his way home Suleyman annexes southern Bessarabia between the Prut and the Dniester. At Bender on the Dniester's western bank he orders Sinan to build a fort to which is fixed a plaque with a writing firm and sure.

I am the slave of Allah, in the government of the world I am Sultan.

Allah made me the follower of the Prophet Muhammad, I who am beloved of the most compassionate one.

God's goodness and Muhammad's miracle-working power are my guides.

In the holy places the sermon was read in my name, in the name of Suleyman.

I am he who makes ships to go to the Frankish Sea, the
    Western Sea and the Indian Sea.
I am the Shah of Baghdad and Iraq, the Emperor of Greece, the
    Sultan of Egypt.
The country, the golden throne and the crown of Hungary are
    in my gift.
He who holds them is the most humble of my slaves . . .
I am Suleyman.

~

Yemen, Prevesa and now Moldavia. Yes, 1538 has been a banner
year.

A rider enters the city and going to all the squares announces
the victory of the Sultan in battle, that all fares well with him,
and that he is on his way home. In the covered market the stall-
holders push their booths far into the alley, decking them with
carpets. The market is adorned with differently patterned,
gilded cloths, pinned together to form a large wall covering.

Against their bolsters sit the shopkeepers, Turks, Greeks,
Jews and Armenians, eating and drinking and playing low-
pitched reed pipes, bagpipes, round timpani with box-shaped
bases, three-stringed lutes not dissimilar to the kind one finds in
Poland and big drums played in the gypsy fashion. For three
days the curfew is suspended and the shops stay open and the
streets are lit even at night so one can walk around as if it were
daytime.

When the Sultan enters the city he is accompanied by Jews
with sweet voices who sing 'blessed be our lord Sultan Suleyman' and toss new coins under the horses' hooves, immediately
retrieved by the Janissaries. The Sultan is preceded by his
beloved elephants who play football and perform other tricks.

The festivities last three days and the people behave as fool-
ishly as Christians do at carnival. Since the Turks drink no wine
but much sherbet, when they do drink wine they like it sweet,
mixed with brandy or honey wine. Some drink until they col-
lapse and cannot walk or speak and are presumed dead. The

truly legless are brought before the judge who sentences them to two hundred blows on the soles, which does wonders for their legs. And a visitor from the north declares that if the Turks, like the Christians, were free to drink wine, they would be the drunkest people in the world.

~

In the New Palace he sits on a domed throne with a handkerchief in his right hand while with his left he gestures in the direction of two pages who offer him a box covered in jewels. Musicians are paired like turtle doves around a central pool: pipers and players of the daf, an orb of stretched hide that is played with the tips of one's fingers, a lutenist and a boy pulling his bow across a piked fiddle.

The Sultan's caftan is a lake of purple silk teeming with swans, gold swans spooling and necking across the chest of their swan-necked master, and when the flasks empty and no lip is dry the music rises to the heavens.

> Come and drink muscatel in the garden, do not believe that
> drunkenness is shameful or against the law for a Frankish
> cupbearer has poured the wine.
> Lover, let not the occasion pass: let not your hand stray from
> the tulip-red wine.

The Sultan's lines.

Act Two: The Haseki

V

Back in the 1490s, when Selim was Governor of Trabzon, the religious judge of that Black Sea port, a certain Omer Efendi, was blessed with a baby son called Yahya. Shortly afterwards the Governor's concubine also gave birth and, looking for a wetnurse, Hafsa entrusted little Suleyman to Omer Efendi's wife. The association between Suleyman and Yahya continued after they had been weaned and they went on to become pupils of a Greek goldsmith called Constantine, a man of great craft and no less severity.

It is no surprise that these two boys who knew the same soft woman and the same hard man ended up friends. That the relationship is strong four decades on, and no longer in the overgrown village of Trabzon, but in Istanbul, is surely connected to the fact that the vocations of Suleyman and Yahya, whom the Sultan addresses even now as 'elder brother', are perfectly opposed, the one being concerned to own the world and the other to reject it.

It's Yahya who enjoys the advantage, because he has something Suleyman wants while the reverse isn't true. Unlike other so-called dervishes whose aura of sanctity is in fact a plea for donations, Yahya's indifference to rank and riches is genuine. If he doesn't approve of something the Sultan does, he tells him in harsh tones and if necessary shuts himself in his dervish lodge and refuses to see him for months as a way of showing his displeasure.

The lodge in question stands high above the Bosporus on land that used to belong to a Greek called Apostol. Once Apostol was caught in a violent storm while sailing and he found himself beseeching the help not of St Nicholas, saint of the seas, but of Yahya the dervish. The storm immediately abated and after safely returning to Istanbul Apostol took his saviour a jug of wine. By the time the jug reached Yahya's lips the wine had turned to pomegranate juice. More than ever convinced of Yahya's divine powers, Apostol gave him land for a lodge among the juniper, mulberry and acacia trees that overlook the strait. Apostol is called Ali now.

Yahya doesn't conceal his friendship with the Prophet Hizir, Moses's companion who drank from the Fountain of Life and became immortal, but for a long time he never acted on Suleyman's hints that he should like to meet him. One day when Suleyman was in the royal barge he sent word for Yahya to join him. Yahya came aboard with an acquaintance and the eyes of the second man were drawn to the Sultan's emerald ring. Suleyman took off the ring and handed it to the man so he might examine it more closely but rather than do so he hurled it into the water. The Sultan said nothing so as not to offend his elder brother, and presently the stranger indicated that he wished to come ashore. As the boat neared land he reached into the water, drew out Suleyman's ring and returned it to him.

After the man had gone Suleyman asked Yahya the meaning of the episode. Yahya replied, 'that was Hizir.'

'Why did you not introduce him to me?' Suleyman demanded. And Yahya replied, 'he tried to make himself known to you, but you did not pay attention.'

~

The word 'harem' derives from the Arabic root *h-r-m* and denotes a place that is prohibited and unlawful as well as one that is sacred, protected and inviolable. Under Islam the area of the home that is set aside for women and children, and certain sacred spaces, such as the interior of a mosque and the sanctuaries of Mecca and Medina, are sufficiently isolated from worldly concerns to be called harems.

In the harem of the New Palace the Sultan has a spy, Gulfem by name. It is possible that she shared his bed but now the relationship is like that of a sister and brother. When she writes to him she includes amusing stories of little consequence, like the story of the bottle of scent he gave her and she mistook for something nice to drink. She knocked it back and her vision darkened, she chattered and gabbled and finally nodded off while the other harem women enjoyed themselves flicking her nose as she slept. 'You should have seen the state of me,' she chides him with the mock-seriousness of a person allowed to take liberties, 'you have made a buffoon of me!'

Turning to the matter at hand, she continues, 'you asked about the woman's expenditure. You swore me to truthfulness and asked about her allowance. I swore her to truthfulness and asked her straight out. She wouldn't tell me. I asked Enver and he told me that she has five hundred florins left. Make of that what you will. The woman isn't aware that I'm telling you this.'

Gulfem and Enver the eunuch are looking out for their mistress, who wasn't born royal and rose thanks to her sweet, quick, attentive nature and well put-together little figure, not her mastery of accounts. So Suleyman sends her five thousand to tide her over and when she complains that her kitchen expenditure is astronomical and her bathroom inadequate he smilingly stumps up more.

~

She was born a simple girl in Ruthenia, the 'Little Russia' of Poland, where she was enslaved by Tatar raiders and sent to Istanbul. Then in an outrageous reversal of fortune she entered the harem and was raised to a position of intimacy with God's vice-regent on earth. Along the way she was renamed Hurrem, which means joyful, smiling or blooming.

Not so simple, after all. No lover of the Sultan has continued to be welcomed into his bed after giving birth to his son. No lover of the Sultan has enjoyed a monopoly over the royal seed, no lover was ever called the Haseki, or Special Friend, no lover has moved into the New Palace, bag and baggage, no lover has been on two thousand aspers a month.

No lover until Hurrem.

In 1520 or thereabouts, when she was first in Suleyman's eye, her rival Mahidevran scratched her face and pulled out her hair in clumps. Hurrem bided her time until she was next called to the Sultan's chamber and he was so moved by her appearance that he banished Mahidevran from his sight forever. Later on when she was threatened by two new girls in the harem she threw herself at the feet of the Sultan's mother, Hafsa of blessed memory, and sobbed so alarmingly that the girls were sent off to provincial marriages.

~

The royal ladies may not be seen. The people espy a carriage coming out of the New Palace and from the size of the escort they guess that it contains Hurrem. They see another carriage enter the palace and their thoughts run to Mihrimah, her only surviving daughter alongside four sons, who is of marriageable age. To gain a fuller picture of the occupants the people rely on former palace eunuchs or ladies-in-waiting, who, after retiring from royal service and coming into the world, plant their observations in the soil of popular curiosity.

That Hurrem isn't beautiful but has charm. That Mahidevran is a stunner who was undone by impetuosity and pride. That Mihrimah has her father eating out of her hand and is the kind of ravishing beauty you sometimes get from a mixing of the races.

Who is close to the people? With whom do we live? With Eyup, the Prophet's brother-in-arms who is now at rest in this city; with immortal Hizir? Aeons and oceans separate us from these heroes but when we speak of them it is as if they are in the next room.

Are the women of the harem not women like us, do they not live with the jinns, as we do, bleed as we bleed, cry as we cry?

~

When she sneezes it is into a handkerchief that has been embroidered with silk and gold and whose border is filled with stars and tulips. Her fingers unclasp a binding made of green jade traced with twists of silver wire and studded with rubies to reveal the miniature Quran within. She slides open a pen box of blue-and-white Iznik ware and withdraws a reed pen, dipping it into a moulded inkwell after removing its small silver cap.

One might ask what the Haseki has that the others don't. The obvious answer, and the one preferred by many of the Sultan's subjects, is that she is a sorceress who has bewitched Suleyman. But sometimes one should look beyond the obvious and specifically to the possibility that she and the Sultan are in love.

When he's away at war surrounded by pyramids of skulls he is grateful to receive a letter in a competent but not learned hand.

'Piece of my heart, felicitous Excellency, my Sultan, from the bottom of my heart, with the longing of one hundred thousand thousand thousand yearnings, with all my heart and all my soul I send you a thousand thousand prayers and praises, I rub my face in the dirt under your feet and kiss your auspicious hand.'

It's nice to be missed. Especially by someone who sympathises with the gout and other aches and pains that come from being an active father of five with executive responsibilities.

Her news is basically his news. 'If you, my Sultan, were to ask after your wretched concubine whose liver is a seared kebab from pain and longing, whose eyes are a flood from separation: God knows, my prosperous one, I spend my every hour in utter distress, and my body moans like a flute from separation. My whole world, my King, God knows that it is impossible to say what I would do just to see your beautiful face. My King, God knows that I burn to a crisp day and night from separation from you. God knows I have not a moment's peace. I am unwell when I am separated from the dirt under your auspicious foot.'

The campaign tent is supposed to be a home from home. But she isn't there. 'I was burned by sorrow when we were apart,' runs one of his poems. 'What shall I do? Oh, what shall I do? I found no remedy for this pain. What shall I do? Oh, what shall I do?'

~

I am the Sultan of Love,
A glass of wine will do
For a crown on my head,
And the brigade of my sighs
Might well serve as the dragon's
Fire-breathing troops.

The bedroom that's best
for you, my love,
Is a bed of roses,
For me, a bed and a pillow
Carved out of rock will do.

My love, take a golden cup
In your hand and drink wine
in the rose garden;
As for me, to sip blood from my heart,
It is enough to have the goblets of your eyes.

If, my beloved, you ride
The horse of coyness,
And trot in the polo grounds,
This head of mine
Will do as a ball for your mallet.

~

She may be seared meat but within the family of seven that she has formed with the Sultan she is supreme. In fact her influence reaches into politics. Of no recent Ottoman consort can this be said, not even Hafsa, who, for all the esteem and affection she enjoyed, was essentially another single-use womb. If Hurrem hasn't quite the status of Maria of Hapsburg, Charles's regent in the Netherlands, or Queen Bona of Poland, who was born into Milan's ducal family, the Sforzas, and fixes alliances for her husband King Sigismund, she has nonetheless entered a category of forward women whose actions have political significance: Queen Catherine of England, for instance, whose principled refusal to accept the invalidity of her marriage to Henry led to his break with the Papacy.

What is more, Hurrem rose without the inherited advantages of these other ladies. She started in chains and without bejewelled relatives to watch out for her. All of which could have been said for Ibrahim the Frank, with the difference that she isn't prone to complacency the way he was. The Frank assumed that the figure he cut in international affairs would protect him from the Sultan's wrath. Big mistake. Celebrity is no substitute for acumen, which means knowing which ear to whisper into and when, and Hurrem has no shortage of that.

No, this woman who puked in a slave ship and snores on the pillow of the most powerful man in the world has the fullest appreciation of what Paolo Giovio likes to call the 'stupefying jokes' that Fortune sometimes plays in raising up a person and throwing that person down again. She's not the kind of girl to contemplate her husband's relative youth, the absence of any life-threatening infirmity, and tell herself, 'there's time.'

She is naturally unavailable for appointment but may be approached through intermediaries. Her current liaison is Stranhila, an inherited asset of the Karaite persuasion. With her Crimean origins and years of service under Hafsa, for whom she would procure military intelligence from foreign ambassadors, Stranhila's job description extends beyond the basic duties of a Jewish handmaiden to source stones and scents. Her rooms in the Old Palace are furnished to the value of twenty-five thousand ducats which when you think about it is nothing for a pair of eyes and ears.

Luxury isn't security. Information is. And connections. The most advantageous feature of the Sultan's harem, more so than its cloisters, courtyards, penthouses, fountains, pergolas trained with vines, its school for maidens who vie for the Haseki's affection, more even than its *objets de luxe*, is its connection to the Sultan. Hurrem need only step through a gate and she is in his Privy Chamber.

When she started out, Ibrahim was ahead of her in Suleyman's affections. But she helped the Sultan to see that the Frank was a threat. The street, the chroniclers and the foreign diplomats all concur on this.

Hurrem was the winner that Ides of March.

~

After some years of concubinage she tells the Mufti, the chief religious authority in the Empire, that she wishes to build facilities for the poor and asks if this will count in her favour on Judgement Day. The Mufti replies that, in view of the fact that she is a slave, credit for these actions will go to her owner the Sultan.

This news makes her anything but joyful, smiling and blooming. For days she cannot be consoled and Suleyman is so worried that he issues her a certificate of manumission. And so, for the first time since she was Aleksandra Lisowska, daughter of a Ruthenian Orthodox priest, she is free.

Free but with ground to make up.

Presently he sends her word: how about it? And Hurrem writes back expressing surprise that he has forgotten God's law prohibiting sex between two free persons outside wedlock. 'While it is perfectly true,' her message reads, 'that in matters of life and death your Highness is a unique and most singular lord in all times, and may resolutely dispose of me in any way you see fit, you cannot, without committing the gravest of sins, couple with me.'

Whether or not a smile plays over Hurrem's lips as the eunuch takes away her message, whether it amuses her to imagine her lover whining like a bloodhound left out of a hunting trip, her rebuttal has the desired effect. In a transport of frustration Suleyman summons the Mufti. The Mufti confirms Hurrem's words. With every passing hour Suleyman's arousal is magnified until his brain supplies the very solution Hurrem has in mind.

Ottoman sultans have been wary of marriage ever since Bayezit I's wife Olivera, daughter of a Serbian princess, was captured along with her husband by Timur the Lame, in 1402, and forced to wait at Timur's table. It was resolved that such a humiliation must never again befall the royal house, but the Ottomans are now all but invincible and it seems odd to base nuptial policy on expectations of defeat.

So it happens that in the year 1536 the people of Istanbul find themselves celebrating the wedding of Suleyman and Hurrem. The streets are illuminated, the houses festooned and everywhere are swings which the people ride with great enjoyment. The blushing bride, pushing thirty-five, with four sons and a daughter, occupies a great tribune in the Hippodrome, from where, screened by a gilt lattice, she and her ladies enjoy a tournament featuring Muslim and Christian knights while tumblers and jugglers and beasts from the Sultan's menagerie, or Lion House, also disport themselves in the arena below.

~

Every Muslim queen should follow the example of Zubayda bint Jafar. She was the granddaughter of al-Mansur, the founder of modern Baghdad, and the wife of the fifth caliph, Harun al-Rashid. She showed an affinity for the sciences, helped the doctors of the law, strengthened the soldiers and comforted the peasants. Her court on the Tigris sounded like a beehive from the number of maidens reciting the Quran day and night. Her son al-Amin, being of royal stock on both sides, was a shoo-in for the caliphate.

The route from Baghdad to Mecca passes through a thousand miles of desert and lava fields, hard going on sandalled feet. Making the pilgrimage in her comfy litter, Zubayda saw the difficulties faced by her less fortunate sisters and brothers, the thirst and exhaustion, the wrong turnings and bleached bones. Recalling that there is no greater act of merit than to enable the poor to fulfil their religious obligations so they can achieve joy in this world and salvation in the next, she ordered improvements.

Zubayda's men cut defiles through mountains, cleared enormous rocks and boulders and built rest stations for pilgrims and beasts of burden. They paved uneven sections and put up milestones marking stages, each one a day's journey of sixteen miles. They bored wells and made reservoirs that collected rainwater and run-off and erected beacons allowing pilgrims to travel in the cool of the night without losing their way. Nor did they leave the new facilities to look after themselves, but replaced pavements when they cracked and kept the beacons supplied with firewood.

On Harun's death al-Amin became caliph but a few years later he was killed by his half-brother al-Mamun, who took the throne but refrained from harassing his stepmother and let her end her days in prayer and solitude. Books of history are filled with that great lady's glory and generosity and even now, seven hundred years after her death, the road to Mecca is known as Zubayda's Way and everyone who passes along it offers thanks to her.

~

The huge Column of Arcadius in the forum of the same name is a relic of old Constantinople. It was built on the Seventh Hill to mark Arcadius's victory over the Goths and it survives even now, its frieze depicting the Emperor in a toga buttoned at the armpit, greaves, bracers and other armaments spiralling up the shaft like the whorl of a shell.

Earthquakes have left deep cracks in the column and it is reported that not long ago several thousand adders, among them an unusually large specimen, came out of the cracks and slithered down to the sea. They were seen by many people who marvelled at the quantity of dust they sent up and the fact that they bit no one during their migration.

Every Sunday there is a market at the foot of the column attended by poor women who each wear a net cap and a small hat, sewn together, and a white cloth which they wrap around their faces like Viennese nuns. From men and women holding scales and drawing their produce out of sacks and baskets the women buy seeds, vegetables and bread that has been kneaded using plain water in the Serbian manner. For this reason the column of Arcadius has come to be known as the Women's Column and its immediate neighbourhood as the Women's Market.

Amid the many excitable accounts that foreigners have written about the Sultan's wealth it is often overlooked that much of the money he gains from waging war is spent waging more war; that some of his subjects are very wretched, living in mud and plank hovels that frequently burn down; and that the assessment of three to four aspers that was levied on every adult male and every married woman after the Moldavian campaign fell on the poor like the rod of Constantine the goldsmith.

Overlooked by many, but not by the Haseki. No longer a spendthrift concubine but a philanthropic queen on the model of Zubayda bint Jafar with a Friday mosque, a primary school, a hospice, a soup kitchen, a seminary and a hospital to build.

The year is 1539. The deeds bear the calligraphic emblem of the Sultan and ground is broken on a large plot behind the Women's Market.

Her dowry of one hundred thousand ducats pays for the initial phases, supplemented by rent from villages that Suleyman has given her and a portfolio that includes shops, rental rooms, caravanserais, bakeries, woodstores, a public bath in the Jewish quarter and, most profitable of all, the double bath she builds near Aya Sofya. Even the revenues from these investments prove insufficient to cover costs and, as as the buildings rise and she engages masons, joiners and tilers in ever-greater numbers, she taps her husband for more funds.

There is a difference between building to the glory of oneself and to the glory of God. The gemstones and sheet gold that Ibrahim the Frank slathered over the New Palace during his upgrade of the late 1520s would be anything but suitable here. Hurrem and her husband's newly appointed chief architect, the same Sinan who got the army across the Prut, strike the right balance and the finished arrangement of arcaded courtyards and lead domelets is dignified and restrained.

The hospital workforce includes physicians, oculists, surgeons, pharmacists, nurses, cleaners, a gardener and administrative staff. The charter that Hurrem draws up to govern the endowment shows her in her best light. The primary school teacher, it stipulates, must treat his charges with the same tenderness as if they were his own children and must not favour one over another. The doctors at the hospital must be 'of noble and generous disposition, good-natured and untroubled. They must demonstrate to every patient the kindness that they would to an intimate friend.' Harsh words are naturally to be avoided, for one such word 'can weigh more heavily on a sick person than the worst of maladies'.

On a site visit, accompanied by female attendants and eunuchs, she looks out from her carriage and is so touched by the plight of the dishevelled and unshod labourers that she sells some of her jewellery to pay for haircuts and shoes.

If you pass the mosque now it's operational you'll hear the voices of thirty men who are paid to sing passages from the Quran that will usher her to paradise at the allotted time. A female scribe takes down the names of children whose mothers wish them to be admitted to the primary school while woodsmoke rising from the chimneys attracts the eligible poor from miles around. Nor must visitors at mealtimes necessarily make do with the standard plain soup that needs rescuing with the addition of lemon juice, vinegar and a little pepper. Twice a week Hurrem's refectory offers meat and on festive occasions diners are treated to luxuries such as butter, saffron, chickpeas, honey, plums, apricots, figs, almonds and currants.

This woman who has it all, five children, a devoted husband and a jewel-encrusted headdress for each day of the week. It's little wonder she is warm of flesh and words, she babbles like one of the streams that run down to the Golden Horn, fast-flowing and ebullient. And yet the status and wealth she has earned by using every atom of her mind and body, the devotion she receives from her family and the laughter of the damsels she pets and mothers, hang by a thread.

VI

In a battle royal the cock birds all fight each other at the same time and the spectators watch keenly knowing that only one will survive. In the Ottoman Empire the fighting cocks are the Sultan's sons and the watchers are his subjects.

The throne doesn't go automatically to the eldest son. This isn't France. Nor is the monarch elected at a meeting of magnates as happens in Hungary. According to an old Turkish belief the selection of a sovereign from among the ruler's sons is the gift of God and to establish a fixed law of succession is to challenge his will. The only requirement is that the candidates be of sound mind and body. This belief was enshrined in law by the present Sultan's great-grandfather, Mehmet the Conqueror, so called because he conquered Constantinople from the Byzantines. The Conqueror might equally be called the Culler because he decreed that 'the one of my sons to whom God grants the sultanate may lawfully put his brothers to death.'

The Conqueror's grandson Selim, Suleyman's father, loved the culling law so much that he expanded it to cover all his male relations. After overthrowing his father Bayezid II in 1512 he made a pretence of sending him off to Dimetoka, near Edirne, but the deposed Sultan never made it to that pleasant retirement spot, having been killed, probably by poison, on the way. Selim pursued one of his brothers to a cave where he was strangled.

Another brother was also strangled. Five nephews ... you get the picture.

When a prince falls his mother falls too. After the Conqueror's death Bayezit beat his brother Cem to the throne and Cem went into exile accompanied by his mother Cicek. When Cem died a decade and a half later his body was repatriated and buried in the former Imperial capital of Bursa, but Cicek never gained readmission to Asia Minor, dead or alive.

~

Hurrem's boys are Mehmet, her eldest, Selim, Bayezit and broke-backed Cihangir. She helped Selim, wriggling and squirming, into an adorable red satin caftan decorated with triple spots in yellow. She fretted for Cihangir and showed doctors his double hunch. Boys who learned and played together and were snipped together and now hunt together. With the exception of Cihangir who is more often than not kept at home for health reasons and is his father's playmate because Suleyman loves the boy's sweetness of temper and quick wit.

When they are old enough Mehmet and Selim accompany Suleyman to war and Hurrem amends her letters accordingly. 'I send a million prayers and praises to Prince Mehmet and Selim,' she writes. 'Your slave Bayezid, your slave Cihangir, your handmaiden Mihrimah rub their faces in the dust beneath your feet.'

Back when she and the Sultan were getting to know each other it seemed like a good idea to have son after son. But what made them happy then will endanger them later on. The present Sultan's father didn't balk at patricide. A precedent one would prefer not to think about.

If it's wrong for a primary school teacher to favour one child over another, what about a mother? By selecting Mehmet she is compassing the murder of Selim and Bayezid, even of poor Cihangir unless he can be spared on compassionate grounds. In moments when the awful realisation strikes her, perhaps she consoles herself with the thought that it's the fault of the law, the fault of her husband, the fault of Mehmet the Conqueror.

Anyone's fault but her own.

~

Mehmet is invited into the Sultan's library where he stands with his hands joined respectfully while his father gestures and makes a point from behind his long writing table. The Prince shows Suleyman the notebook that he has filled with copies of the Sultan's own poems, not without mistakes or crossings out, some of the words carrying diacritical marks that indicate a passing acquaintance with something called grammar.

When his father is away bashing unbelievers Mehmet writes to him with the easy informality of a boy who is well loved.

'If you ask about my mother,' runs one letter, 'everything is fine for now. Undoubtedly because she is separated from you, her body is not completely healthy and she longs for you, and day and night her moans fill this transient existence. May it please God that you destroy the enemy and return as soon as possible.' The Prince reports that he is making progress reading Menavino's travelogue.

Elsewhere he thanks Suleyman for indulging his request that a certain servant be promoted to a high position. But he is troubled by his father's excessive reliance on the opinion of others. 'I ask that you not be swayed by anyone's words,' is the sage advice of this twelve-year-old to the Master of the Celestial Conjunction.

He's a newshound. 'Since that time the city burned at night it has caught fire a further twelve times, but on each occasion they were informed early and put out the fire.' By 'they' he means the Janissaries who alone have the authority to fight fires, the grappling hooks needed to pull down houses and the insolence to enter evacuated homes and help themselves to whatever they want.

In a happier vein, he continues, 'my dear Sultan, a navy of infidels was sent against Hayreddin Pasha. Through the favour of Allah ... he fought and defeated the infidel, captured one hundred and eighty galleys and buried the remainder in the waters of the sea.'

Not long ago, at the hunting ground on the banks of the Maritsa, he and Selim engaged in chatter about fabled Rustem's achievement in shooting an arrow through a knot of branches to kill his treacherous brother Shaghad. From Rustem the conversation moved on to Bahram who was so successful a hunter of the wild ass, or *gur*, that he was nicknamed Bahram Gur. Irked by his sons' praise of sportsmen other than himself, the Sultan ordered three wild boars to be driven towards him and, riding abreast of them, shot a single arrow that passed through all three and lodged in the tree behind.

~

In 1504 twelve-year-old Giovanantonio Menavino was voyaging with his father, a Genoese merchant, when they were seized by pirates and the boy was brought to Sultan Bayezit in the New Palace. Much taken by his young guest, Bayezit ordered him to be fed. Looking for somewhere to sit, unaware that the Turks eat on the floor, Giovanantonio took his plate and, as he writes in *Five Books on the Laws, Religion and Way of Life of the Turks*, 'made a seat on a staircase not far away, which soon led to laughter from those around me, and from the Grand Turk'. Then he was taken to the Old Palace, where the harem was in those days, washed with hot water seasoned with herbs and dressed in green satin and brocade breeches in the Turkish fashion, that is to say, three palms in length, before being brought back to the Sultan.

Kissing Bayezit's hand and seeing 'the place and the time to be opportune,' Giovanantonio broached the plight of his father from whom he had been separated following their capture. Bayezit gave orders for the elder Menavino to be found but he had already been sold on, leaving no trace. Giovanantonio entered royal service as a companion to the Sultan's nephews. 'I began to read the alphabet; and for four years I studied their

Turkish language, literary and vulgar, going on to some books in Arabic, and some in Persian.' And thus, 'in the course of continuous studies and vigils ... I fully learned all their laws, prayers [and] sacrifices.'

No reader of the *Five Books,* and certainly no young man with a loving father, could fail to rejoice with Giovanantonio when he learns that Genoese merchants had bought the freedom of the elder Menavino in deepest Anatolia. 'He came to the great city of Constantinople to find me,' the boy continues, 'and knowing I was in the Palace, arranged to come and meet me and seeing me in that good health in which he had left me, was greatly consoled.' Bayezit's daughters prevailed on the Sultan to let Giovanantonio spend some days with his father before the old man returned to Genoa, after which the boy 'stayed for a period of five years in that same Palace, without having ... news from home.'

Five Books would not be available for the Sultan's sons to read if this tragic tale of family severance hadn't ended happily. Pressed into the army of Sultan Selim during the Iran campaign of 1514, Giovanantonio deserted and after an arduous voyage made it back to Genoa. 'I found my father and my dear mother, but they, thinking I must be dead, marvelled greatly and as if they had acquired me once again, encircled me weeping with excessive joy; whom I embraced and kissed tenderly.'

~

An episode whose significance only increases with the passage of time. It is the summer of 1530. Hurrem sits on a latticed terrace overlooking the Hippodrome. The Sultan's three elder sons are to be exhibited to the public at the climax of festivities marking their circumcision.

When the Princes ride into that great arena, the eyes of Hurrem the mother rush to Mehmet, just eight years of age, in his satin jacket of pale limoncello, and to Selim, three years his junior, dangerously adorable and equipped with a baby scimitar encrusted with gems.

All the while the eyes of Hurrem the politician are on the third boy, Mahidevran's twelve-year-old son Mustafa. This pale, handsome youth, who has his father's swan-like neck, is dressed in a long, loose Turkish mantle of crimson satin under a velvet caftan of the same colour with a golden hem adorned with jewels.

It is claimed that Mustafa is beloved of the Janissaries. They have loved him ever since he was a little boy when he performed astonishing athletic feats in and out of the saddle. Claims that are about to be tested for the Janissaries are massed on the Hippodrome floor.

The Janissary Corps makes and breaks sultans. They weighed in decisively for Bayezit in 1481. Three decades later they overthrew him in favour of Selim. The first thing Suleyman did on becoming Sultan was buy their love at three thousand aspers a heart. Which didn't stop them hating Ibrahim the Frank and trashing his palace. Now they hate Hurrem because she has enchanted the Sultan and relieved him of his cock and both his balls. If they had their way they would pack her off to Bursa, junkyard for concubines as well as graveyard for pretenders, and reinstate Mahidevran to her rightful place as the most senior of the Sultan's women.

When the Sultan's sons come face to face with the Janissaries in the Hippodrome that day, it's an indicative moment, a political moment. The crowd see it, the foreign visitors see it, Hurrem sees it. Mahidevran, also in attendance, also hidden from view, sees it.

And the Janissaries do what Hurrem would have them not do. Ignoring her sons they direct their passion and affection only at Mustafa. And he, showing a fine instinct for gesture, inclines his head towards them as he has seen his father do many times.

~

When the sons of a sultan grow up they are sent off to become governor of a province. They are usually accompanied by their mother who keeps house for them. This is what Hafsa did for young Suleyman. They each have a tutor who teaches them how to govern. At least that's the theory. In reality it's not unknown for young princes to go astray. Alemsah, for example, another of Bayezit's sons, excelled at staying drunk for weeks and at spending his mother's allowance.

In truth whatever a prince learns in his province is less important than where he learns it. Provincial governorships are desirable only to the extent that they offer easy access to the capital when the Sultan dies and there is the inevitable dash to claim the throne. Manisa is coveted because it is only five days from Istanbul. No one wants Amasya because it is halfway to Iran. Konya is somewhere in between.

~

In the spring of 1533 Mustafa comes up the Council Road to the New Palace from his home in the Old. Handsomer than ever, already taller than his father, his moustaches are beginning to go from sparse and blond to thick and dark. He is dressed in gold and has a tulip-shaped turban studded with gems. After taking leave of the Sultan he does a turn on horseback for the crowd, offering a most pleasing sight.

His caravan to Manisa goes west, by road to the coast and then southwards by ship, past Chios with its famous tears, carrying his satins and velvets, his gold and silver plate and four hundred thousand aspers to be getting on with – for all the world a sultan, not a sultan's fifteen-year-old son.

When Suleyman was Governor of Manisa, Mahidevran was one of seventeen women in his harem. She was outranked by three others who earned five aspers a day to her four. Mustafa's birth turned her from a jobbing concubine into the mother of the future Sultan.

Having returned to the same city with Mustafa, the establishment she runs for him is bigger than the courts of many kings. The civilian side comprises Mustafa's tutor, personal steward and treasurer as well as chancery and kitchen staff, pages, houndsmen, falconers, stable boys, craftsmen, doctors and personal attendants. There are also several divisions of cavalry, standard-bearers, tent-pitchers and musicians. The stewards of the Prince's harem supervise the concubines and their ladies-in-waiting. Hangers-on include writers and artists, creative types of irregular income who have attached themselves to the handsome prince.

On Fridays he goes to the mosque preceded by forty soldiers on horseback as well as archers, nine in number, each archer wearing a long white shirt and carrying a bow and fifty arrows. When the horsemen reach the door of the mosque they stand in two lines forming a corridor along which passes the Prince accompanied by his tutor, an old man with a white beard. As they go past the soldiers cry 'May God prolong the life of the Sultan!' and bow their heads.

Opposite the gate that is set into the earth wall encircling the Prince's residence is a square for equestrian training and in the middle of the square there is a tall mast of wood surmounted by an apple of gilded copper. Nobody is as skilled as Prince Mustafa at hitting this apple with an arrow while riding at a gallop.

Whether it's his own sense of what's good for him or the influence of Mahidevran who regrets her earlier impulsiveness, the Prince takes pains to avoid giving his father any cause for complaint or suspicion. In a letter to the New Palace he assures 'the audience chamber of the shadow of God of the orbit of the world which is the altar of the renowned sultans and lords of destiny' that this 'insubstantial worthless dust-like atom' is 'continually engaged in learning the religious sciences and perfecting the elements of divine prosperity.' Translated into ordinary Turkish this means: Dad, I'm buried in my books.

On the available evidence, if he becomes sultan Mustafa will make a good all-rounder in the mould of his father. He's no tyrant and if a preacher speaks against him he doesn't have him killed but simply bans him from the pulpit. He's generous, and any government official passing through Manisa receives his hospitality and leaves his territory praising him. Alongside his martial interests he enjoys the company of poets whose verses, big on roses and nightingales, agree with the bucolic side of his personality. He keeps a cellar and is the father of a baby girl, Nergissah Sultan, which suggests that he has a good work–life balance.

When he was a child Mustafa was jealous of Suleyman's love for Ibrahim the Frank and made his feelings known. Later he realised that it wasn't the Frank but his own brothers he needed to guard against. When Ibrahim's power was at its peak, he and his wife Muhsine cultivated the friendship of Mahidevran. In the course of a military campaign Ibrahim sent Mustafa a report in which he called himself the Prince's 'sincere friend' and expressed his desire to 'take profit from and be gladdened by [Mustafa's] noble and blessed grace'.

Even now that Ibrahim is dead, Mustafa and his mother are not without allies. Lutfi Pasha, the Sultan's brother-in-law and the Second Vizier, for instance, has been blocking Hurrem's attempts to have the Prince and his mother transferred from Manisa to somewhere further from the capital. Which demonstrates the Haseki's need for a political champion if she is to engineer the succession of one of her sons. Now, how exactly does a sultan's wife acquire a grand vizier?

~

Rustem's family name used to be Opukovic. He started his career as a pig-driver in a village in Bosnia. His father gave him and his brother to the government in lieu of the poll tax that must be paid by the Sultan's non-Muslim subjects.

Even then he was small, ugly and red. Only a sense of humour can have led the officers who took him into the Sultan's service to name him after an Iranian warrior and hunter of legendary beauty. Resourceful and intelligent, Rustem won entry to the most prestigious royal preparatory school before becoming a page in the Third Court of the New Palace.

One day Suleyman was standing at a window when something fell from his hand. The other pages scattered in pursuit of the object, sprinting through doorways and careening down staircases. Rustem dropped coolly from the window ledge onto the pavement below and, picking up the object, returned it to its owner who saw something in this fellow and appointed him to the Privy Chamber.

In due course Rustem became the Sultan's sword-holder. Only the head of the Privy Chamber, the office that until recently was held by Hadim Suleyman, and was inaccessible to Rustem for obvious reasons, outranked him.

In 1526, in his mid twenties, Rustem was released from the Third Court and became master of the Sultan's stable. Planning the equine families that carry the Ottoman one, managing farms that supply fodder, overseeing the Sultan's smiths and grooms, saddlers and housing-makers.

Being a horsey person Suleyman consulted his stablemaster frequently and was much taken with his intelligence, loyalty, piety, politeness and sobriety. Only Rustem's avarice, a quality often found in swineherds, displeased him. Yet might not this vice, if employed in his master's interest, become a virtue?

In 1533, when Ibrahim the Frank was wintering in Aleppo, his spies back home sent word that the Sultan was allowing Rustem liberties and praising him lavishly. That sounded ominously similar to Ibrahim's own experience ten years earlier, so he appointed Rustem to be Governor of the distant province of Diyarbakir. When Rustem complained about his exile the Sultan could only reply, 'when I see Ibrahim I will see about getting you sent back to my side.' Which pretty much summed up his powerlessness over his own government in those days.

~

What about Rustem? the Sultan asks.

What about him? Apart from the fact that he's twice Mihrimah's age and ugly, while Davud Pasha, the Governor of Egypt, is young and handsome. So answers Hurrem.

Finding Suleyman sold on Rustem, Hurrem has a word with her husband's doctor. Moses Hamon is the son of Joseph Hamon, a native of Grenada, who was expelled under the Inquisition and entered Selim's service as his campaign doctor. Moses obligingly puts it about that the reason Rustem is so red is that he suffers from the French disease. A deal-breaker if ever there was one. But there are limits even to Suleyman's flexibility and he tells another doctor, a certain Mehmet, to ride across Anatolia to Diyarbakir where Mehmet orders the Governor to strip naked and going over his body disturbs a louse living comfortably amid the folds.

It is well known that lice don't settle on syphilitic bodies. And so a smiling Mehmet announces to Rustem that this little squirmer shouldn't be mistaken for a louse. It is the hand in marriage of the Sultan's only daughter.

~

On the night of 3 July 1539 a fire breaks out in a shop that sells pitch at the port of Istanbul. It consumes the nearby prison along with seven hundred inmates. The flames leap across the Golden Horn and up the hill to the markets of Tahtakale. The city's provisions of lard, broad beans, peas, rice and flax go to cinders. The Pashas arrive and the whole world arrives and the Janissaries tear down houses downwind of the fire which burns on till the following evening.

Eight days later the Grand Vizier dies of the plague. Ayas the Albanian whose three brothers are in Catholic orders at Avlona. Ayas the mega-fecund. At the peak of his potency forty cots were counted in his palace and he leaves behind one hundred and thirty children.

Ibrahim the Frank was appointed to the top job without having to scroll through the lesser vizierates. The Sultan won't make that mistake again. So when Lutfi Pasha, his brother-in-law, is promoted from Second to Grand, Hadim Suleyman goes from Third to Second and a former Governor of Rumelia from Fourth to Third.

Which leaves a vacancy at Fourth. Conveniently for Hurrem who doesn't want to lose her daughter to the provinces, for Mihrimah, who feels the same way, and for Suleyman who had Rustem down as ministerial material all along.

VII

Between two extremes there is a middle, observes the Venetian ambassador to the French court, when Francis and Charles show signs of settling their differences. 'These two princes,' he reports to his masters back home on the Lagoon, 'hitherto so full of mistrust and such excessive hatred for each other that the one could not speak of the other without ... odious words, have retreated from these extremes; their conduct softens by the day and their aversion cools.'

In June 1538 Queen Eleanor, Francis's wife and Charles's sister, travels by ship to meet the Emperor after an interval of many years. As she disembarks onto a wooden pier erected for the occasion he advances and embraces her and in this way the siblings remain for some time until such a crowd of people has assembled that the pier gives way and everyone is pitched into the shallows. Much laughter and a change of clothes later, the Queen relates to her brother how matters stand between Francis and one of her ladies, Madame d'Etampes, and begs him to pay court to her in public, upon which the Emperor rises and, with the intention of embarrassing Madame d'Etampes, embraces her saying that he wishes very much to become the object of her affections, surpassing even King Francis.

The Emperor pays Francis a visit in December of the following year. In the Loire Valley he is met by the King who presents him with a suit of clothes worth forty thousand ducats, which

Charles declines on the grounds that he is mourning his wife Isabella who died recently after giving birth to yet another still-born child. After a day's hunting at Amboise the party enters a tower in the chateau with a ramp inside that lets the horses ascend to the roof, but the lamps fill the tower with flames and smoke, panicking the horses and almost asphyxiating their riders. Francis, his eyes rolling furiously, gives orders that those responsible should be hanged and it takes all Charles's powers of persuasion to convince him to relent.

On New Year's Day, 1540, the Emperor enters Paris and is greeted by cheering crowds, 'peace' and 'concord' being the themes of the decorations on his route. And Francis, who fif-teen years ago was in a foetid prison in Madrid, puts up his former gaoler in the splendour of the Louvre. 'We have been so well-treated and feted,' Charles notes, his grief apparently sur-mountable, 'we spend all our days hunting and hawking and the nights whirling and dancing until it is time for bed.'

~

The Sultan is unsettled by the news that his French ally and Hapsburg enemy are now brothers and by claims that Francis, Charles and the Pope, 'enjoying the common support of all the other princes and potentates of Christianity, have concluded . . . that [Francis] will be crowned Emperor of Constantinople . . .' So reports Antonio Rincon, the most adroit of the diplomats who are making careers by mediating, leveraging and otherwise exploiting the relationship between the Ottoman Empire and Christendom.

Rincon was born at Medina del Campo, in Castile, and he started his career in Charles's household. In 1520 he joined a Castilian revolt in the course of which the government burned Medina del Campo to the ground. Confirmed in his hatred of his former master, disqualified from a military career by the rolls of flab that swathe his midriff, Rincon became a diplomat for the King of France.

Since then he has made himself popular in jurisdictions in

Eastern Europe that decline to be swallowed by Archduke Ferdinand while taking money and a steer from the French. At the court of Hungary's on–off king, Janos Zapolya, Rincon is received, as he himself puts it, 'as if I had come from heaven'. He charms Poland with the same easy urbanity as he charms Venice. And he has a knack of evading the Hapsburg brothers whose territory he crosses with impunity.

An ambassador of the Most Christian King must carry a certain authority for his age and be always ready to invent, propose and respond to the needs of the moment. He must speak Italian, the language of bribery, otherwise he will not be made welcome and will be unable to maintain the grandeur of France.

It was Rincon who laid the foundations for Francis's Turkish alliance and the Sultan greets him with artillery salutes. Opening his luggage, he presents Lutfi Pasha with an exquisite globe of Venetian construction worth one hundred and fifty thousand crowns. The Sultan's doctor Moses Hamon receives a gold chain, the junior Pashas robes of silk and the porter a few coins. Rincon's generosity extends to everyone who shows him kindness and is more than repaid in the intelligence – fleet movements, bowel movements – he receives in return.

If the Porte's suspicions of Christian insincerity cannot be laid to rest, they must be put to use. With his usual dexterity Rincon intimates that the Emperor's hawking and whirling in France doesn't amount to a peace, far less an alliance, but only an intermission. And in due course the parties appear to corroborate his scepticism, Francis showing no sign of giving up Burgundy and Charles making Milan over to his son Philip.

The friendship between the Most Christian King and the Sultan is like a ring that cannot be removed from the finger except by cutting it off. So says Rincon. But a hand has more than one finger and often more than one ring. It would be to Suleyman's as well as Francis's advantage if the Republic of Venice were drawn away from Charles. And the Serenissima, disadvantaged by her ill-advised participation in the Holy League and still fuming at Doria's treachery, is keen.

Enter Rincon with his measuring stick and the peace he runs up between the Sultan and the Doge has the additional advantage of showing the world how far Venice has fallen in the Sultan's affections and how completely France has become Hurrem to the Serenissima's Mahidevran! So humiliating is the treaty to Venice, so complete the picture of decline, that in addition to confirming the earlier loss of colonies to Barbarossa's naval forces it obliges her to give up her two remaining trading posts in the Peloponnese and to pay the Porte three hundred thousand ducats, bad enough at the best of times but excruciating in a famine.

~

The Hapsburg heartland runs from the Baltic to the Danube. Further west, Maria of Hapsburg governs the Netherlands while Ferdinand is responsible for Germany, Bohemia, Austria and Hungary, though his ownership of the kingdom of Hungary is largely aspirational, much of it lying in the hands of the Sultan's client Janos Zapolya. Charles, while caring very much for his patrimony, cares even more for his maritime ventures against the Turk. He is planning, he says, to raise sixty thousand men and as many ships as may be necessary for the liberation of Constantinople, 'which is surrounded by sea on three sides, via the Dardanelles, which I am told can be captured easily'.

Not so easily, warns his sister Maria. 'Even if the campaign starts so well that Your Majesty wins some town and begins to advance,' she writes, 'if you lack the means to press on, think what a disgrace and cause for regret it would be . . . Your Majesty's task is to vanquish, not to be vanquished.' Chastened, her brother decides on the more achievable prize of Algiers, Barbarossa's North African base of operations from which he raids the coasts of Spain.

An illusion of compromise continues to beguile the Emperor into believing that with a little reform here, a dose of theological compromise there, Rome and Luther will be reconciled. But it is harder to find a universally acceptable definition for the word 'transubstantiation' than one might think. A Church council proving impossible, in June 1540 Charles presides over a modest colloquy at one of his palaces near the Rhine. Luther stays away citing security concerns and all that is produced is 'smoke and great confusion', in the words of a French diplomat familiar with proceedings.

Luther's recent treatises lay stress on Pope Paul's transvestism and penchant for vomiting devils. 'The spirit of Antichrist is the Pope,' he contends, 'his flesh is the Turk. One attacks the Church physically, the other spiritually. Both however are of one lord, the devil, since the Pope is a liar and the Turk a murderer.' To Luther the so-called 'holy war' that the Pope keeps calling for is a contradiction in terms. The Turks are to be endured like floods, forest fires, plagues and famines, all sent by God to try his people. Not that Luther is blind to the Turks' good points, which apparently include their obedient women and distaste for ostentation. Evidently Brother Martin doesn't know the Haseki and has yet to attend a week-long Ottoman circumcision party!

That the principal agent of division in Europe is demanding a united front against the Turk is an irony much savoured by the Sultan, who tells a visitor that if Luther was a bit younger he 'would have found in me a gracious lord'. The Caliph of Islam and the monk of Wittenberg are in each other's debt as it is. Whenever Suleyman marches north the Hapsburg brothers are obliged to make concessions to the Lutherans in return for contributions to the common defence. And the heresy is the biggest obstacle to the formation of a Christian force capable of liberating Constantinople. So when Luther, hearing what Suleyman has been saying about him, crosses himself and murmurs, 'God protect me from this gracious lord!' he is perhaps being less than sincere.

～

Hungary is the curtain wall of Christendom. The Hungarian throne has long been claimed by Ferdinand, while Suleyman, who installed King Janos as his tributary, thus denying himself the opportunity to enjoy the kingdom's mines and forests, its leather, fleeces, wine and grain, has on occasion regretted his generosity and considered making it formally his.

On 22 July 1540 Janos dies leaving a twenty-one-year-old widow, Isabella, daughter of King Sigismund of Poland and Queen Bona, and a fourteen-day-old heir who is named Stephen after the saint of that name who was Hungary's first king.

The Sultan sends a state messenger to Buda, the capital, to congratulate the mother and inspect the child. During the audience Stephen arches and puckers and Isabella takes out a breast and suckles him. Moved by this scene of maternal tenderness, the state messenger drops to his knees and swears in the Sultan's name that when Stephen becomes a man, he, and only he, will reign over Hungary. The bill for recognition comes to three hundred thousand ecus from the Hungarian treasury.

That autumn Ferdinand's Polish fixer Jerome Laski arrives in Istanbul to persuade Suleyman to rescind recognition and give Hungary to his master in return for an annual tribute. He passes on this demand even though it is well known that Suleyman doesn't do withdrawals, only acquisitions. The gifts that the Pole brings with him, falcons for the Sultan, velvets, damasks and sable skins for the Pashas, had better land.

A few years ago Laski was in town negotiating Hungary's submission to the Porte in return for its protection from Ferdinand. That he is now pursuing the opposite objective would be funny if it wasn't so tawdry, predictable and Christian. In Laski's meeting with the Pashas, Lutfi raises the question of transferable loyalties and the Pole replies that there is in Constantinople at this moment a certain Castilian ambassador of the King of France 'who lives not as a Spaniard but as a Frenchman, therefore we Christians are free to serve whomsoever we will'. He is referring to Antonio Rincon who is keeping tabs on Laski and outspending him to make sure his mission fails.

'You see that you are now in our possession,' Lutfi goes on unpleasantly, 'why not reveal to us the power of the King of the

Germans, and whether he has great treasures?' By the King of the Germans he means Ferdinand. And Laski, after noting that some princes play down their wealth in order to extract more from the people while others exaggerate it the better to intimidate their enemies, puts Ferdinand's revenue from Austria, Bohemia, Tyrol and the Rhine at a little over two million.

A figure that delights Lutfi. 'The Sultan receives this amount from Cairo alone!' And so the conversation goes, both men trying to convince the other that his master has the bigger dick, until Laski, returning to the question at hand, declares that he has come to Constantinople to 'make a good and firm peace, and establish a better friendship'. To the Pole's embarrassment his words are immediately contradicted by news that an army sent by Ferdinand is at this moment besieging Queen Isabella and her infant in Buda Castle.

The Sultan has two ways of showing anger. The first is to bawl the offender out of his presence. The second is to sit very still with his hand over his chest until the object of his ire looks for the nearest hole. With Laski it is the first. 'Why,' Suleyman demands when he receives the Pole on 7 November, 'did [Ferdinand] send an army into my kingdom, and why did you even come here, and where is your honour now that your king is trying to deceive me?' All this put into Latin by his chief translator, the tall, consummate, eminently bribable Yunus Bey, who spends his life on ships or with his mouth over the Sultan's ear.

Now Suleyman waves Yunus away and shouts in Turkish and it's clear from the reactions of the Pashas, who fix their eyes on the floor, that they don't often see him this cross. Laski is taken away to prison and the Sultan resolves to send a relief force to lift the siege of Buda pending a full-scale invasion. Later on Laski learns that Hadim Suleyman, who evidently retains an interest in mutilation, suggested that the Pole's ears and nose be sent to Ferdinand and that the Sultan was only dissuaded from this course of action by the excellence of his falcons.

~

'The French ambassador has set out for [the court of] the King of France,' Laski informs Ferdinand in a letter sent from behind bars, 'to exhort him to make war against … the Emperor.' So precious are the contents of the head of Antonio Rincon that the Senators of Venice, who are bound by treaty to the Ottomans and the French and fear that he will be abducted while passing through their territory, assign him a guard of fifty men-at-arms.

At Blois he is feted by Francis, honoured with a lordship on the River Saone and given fresh instructions. On 8 May, 1541 he begins the return journey to Constantinople in the company of Cesar Fregoso, a Genoese noble who has also defected to Francis and whose armed guard will escort them as far as Venice before Rincon goes on alone to Constantinople. On 1 July in French-held Piedmont the local Governor informs the travellers that the Marquis of Vasto, who administers neighbouring Milan for the Emperor, has put agents along the River Po. The Po is not the only route to Venice from north-western Italy but it is well known that Rincon is inconvenienced by his girth and prefers a leisurely cruise to wobbling along the bridle paths.

To confuse Vasto's spies the ambassadors' goods and servants are embarked on a separate boat and a dozen horsemen are sent ahead as decoys. Rincon also hands over his instructions so they are not on his person. At midnight on 2 July he and Fregoso push off downstream and travel through the night. Vasto's men are in three boats, tied alongshore, which they have camouflaged using leaves and branches. And at midday on 3 July, shortly after they enter Milanese territory, the ambassadors are intercepted.

Six days later Rincon's valet and secretary arrive at Venice holding his instructions. But where is the Excellency to whom they were entrusted? Reports come in suggesting that Rincon and Fregoso are being questioned by the Emperor himself and others that he has been imprisoned in Milan. Fregoso's wife learns that he is safe and in a custody not devoid of comfort but that Rincon is being kept under worse conditions.

On 28 July the Emperor brings an imperial diet to a close and rides over the Alps to Milan. At the cathedral font he takes Vasto's son in his arms, becoming his godfather. Expressing dismay at events on the Po, he appoints a special investigator to 'locate and liberate' the missing men. He swears on the soul of the late Empress that he knows nothing of their whereabouts. But he knows that the ambassadors are already dead and when Vasto requests his permission for their assassins to escape from the prison where they are being kept, it is granted.

The moral high ground is unfamiliar territory to the Most Christian King but no less congenial for that. 'The emperor,' he intones, 'has committed an injury so great, so execrable and so strange towards humankind . . . that it cannot ever be forgotten, suffered or tolerated: namely that by means of some of his ministers, our ambassadors . . . were treacherously and inhumanly assassinated and killed as they were on their way to Venice on our business . . . In this, the emperor acted against the truce negotiated between him and me – something repugnant to all divine and human law, and contrary to the ancient and settled custom established between kings and princes, states and republics, from the creation of the world until now.'

Having been unsettled by the Franco-Hapsburg rapprochement, no one is more delighted than the Sultan by its demise. The irony is that by murdering Rincon, Charles has furthered two objectives, the end of his detente with Francis and the strengthening of Turco-French amity, that the ambassador was trying to achieve all along.

VIII

Buda sits on high ground amid fertile country. To one side it is bordered by vine-clad hills while on the other it commands a view of the Danube with its various islands and the village of Pest on the opposite bank, communicable by pontoon. The city used to be adorned with the palaces of the Hungarian nobility, some of which burned down when Suleyman set the city alight after his invasion of 1526, while others are kept from falling by a liberal use of props and stays. The former seat of Matthias Corvinus, the last Hungarian king strong enough to intimidate Ottomans and Hapsburgs alike, has seen better days.

The Dowager Queen Isabella is beautiful with a touch of Milan. Schooled in the humanist way back in Krakow, conversant in Polish, Latin, German and Italian, her brief marriage to King Janos has left her with little more than the rings on her fingers and the infant in her lap. Whether she survives her change of circumstance depends on how she handles the bullies to the south and the north. It also depends on how she handles her house bully, George Martinuzzi, or 'Brother George', as he likes to be known. Janos's former treasurer and the Bishop of Oradea, one of the kingdom's richest sees, has assumed the regency pending Stephen's majority.

Brother George started out stoking fires back in Croatia and only learned to read and write after entering a monastery in his mid twenties. In the 1520s he became Janos's fixer, smoothing his path to the throne and arranging his marriage. If Brother George's attitude towards Hungary's neighbours seems contradictory, if his protestations of devotion to Ferdinand sit oddly with the stream of information he provides Suleyman, this is because he understands that between two powerful neighbours all one can hope to do is kick up dust. Above all Brother George wishes to augment his influence over the dowager Queen.

When he hears about Janos's death, Ferdinand sends his ambassador Nicholas von Salm, son of the Nicholas von Salm who led the successful defence of Vienna when Suleyman tried to invade in 1529, with instructions to offer Isabella cash and her son a fiefdom further north if she will give Ferdinand the throne. He is met by Brother George who greets the envoy with a shake of the head, an audience being sadly out of the question on account of the Queen's debilitating and all-consuming grief.

When she hears about Brother George's attempt to marginalise her, Isabella threatens to kill herself which persuades the regent to revise his diagnosis, and von Salm is hurriedly shown in. Wearing no jewellery, her cheeks pale and her eyes tired but showing no inclination to cry, the Queen sits on a hard bed in a room draped with dark fabrics, the windows blacked out to prevent the entry of any cheering light. And this girl whose ailment is actually a debilitating and all-consuming case of older men pleads for more time to consult her father King Sigismund, noting that it would be a great dishonour for Ferdinand to send an army against a widow in her weeds and a baby in his cot.

The invasion that Ferdinand launches in the autumn of 1540 is repulsed. The following summer a more powerful Hapsburg force, this one under Wilhelm von Roggendorf, another veteran of Vienna, lays siege to Buda. The defence is led by Brother George who is everywhere repairing walls and preaching the virtue of hunger as the siege drags into June and food stocks dwindle; he is to the embattled Hungarians what the doughty Antonio da Silveira was to the defenders of Diu. Roggendorf's frustration is compounded by memories of his earlier, unsuccessful assault on the city, in 1530, when the defenders included a younger Martinuzzi. And Brother George, who has exchanged his white habit for helmet and cuirass, taunts this 'stupid old man who has come to meet his death in the same ditches where he was previously humiliated,' asking only that the Austrian load his guns with lighter ordnance to avoid disturbing his pregnant sow back home.

In June an Ottoman relief force commanded by the Governor of Belgrade arrives and the siege is lifted. Close behind is the much larger army of the Sultan along with an ailing Jerome Laski who has been dragged all the way from Istanbul because no one can think what else to do with him. Roggendorf deploys his men in defensive positions on the Hill of St Gerard, where the saint of that name was rolled to his death, and not far from hot baths which accommodate a species of golden scaled fish that if put into the Danube die immediately. A Hapsburg garrison on the island of Csepel, which commands the plain by which Suleyman's army is approaching, is put to the sword.

There are no good options if the Ottoman Sultan is bearing down on you with one hundred thousand men. On 25 August Roggendorf looks for an escape across the Danube. Lashing his barges to the bridge the better to transfer his heavy guns, he waits for nightfall but a storm arises that tears through the pontoons and scatters the ships. Caught between the foaming Turk and the raging river, the Hapsburgs crowd onto what vessels remain, capsizing with results familiar to the fish with the golden scales. Martinuzzi orders hay stores in the Austrian camp to be set on fire and by their dreadful light the surviving Austrians are shot from the shore. News of the massacre reaches the Sultan, downstream, in the form of a regatta of corpses.

Arriving in the city, Suleyman occupies the hill with the finest prospect and gives orders that eight hundred Hungarians who fought for Roggendorf and were taken prisoner be executed. The clemency he shows Jerome Laski comes too late for the Pole who dies shortly after he is given his freedom, Roggendorf also succumbing to his wounds.

Inside the city walls the church of St Mary is cleansed of

sculptures, paintings and other evidence of idolatry, and a pulpit and prayer niche are installed. The poor women of Buda, whose hovels lean close to the mosque entrance, gather to glimpse Suleyman as he emerges after Friday prayers. When his chief secretary enquires what they are saying, the translator replies that the sound of Muslim prayers being chanted is not foreign to them, on the contrary, these mellifluous tones were heard in Janos's time but no one knew where they came from, as if the building was a mosque all along and was waiting for the Refuge of the Caliphate to reveal it as one.

~

On 28 August the Refuge of the Caliphate sends Queen Isabella three horses with harnesses and bridles of gold, saddles set with precious stones and four dresses of woven gold. Regretting that the statutes of his empire do not allow him to visit her in person, he asks that her boy be brought to his camp to be kissed by this sincere friend of his father the late king.

'The Sublime Porte is open to all.' So runs the Ottoman saying. But there are many who, having gained admission, are waiting to leave. Take the case of Peter Perenyi, a Hungarian noble whose son was entrusted to the Sultan only to find himself circumcised and inducted into the ranks of the pages of the Third Court! The state messenger's promise that Buda will be in trust only until Stephen is old enough to take up his functions . . . well, a lot can happen over the course of a childhood. So the Sultan's invitation causes understandable anxiety in the young Queen.

And Brother George assures her that whatever else might be said of the Grand Turk, he is a religious person who will keep his word and also a man easily offended whose army is outside the window.

On 29 August Isabella allows Stephen to be brought out of the city by a wetnurse and two nannies, the infant and the women in a golden coach and Brother George and his fellow councillors on foot. The Sultan's camp is encircled by a ditch defended by a barricade of wagons and cannons linked by chains, behind which stands a line of camels. Rustem greets the Hungarians and escorts them to the Sultan's tent, which is impossible to miss, in part because of its size, in part because of the quality of the soldiers around it.

At the threshold the king exercises his lungs which alarms the men who are present and it falls to the wetnurse to carry him in. Suleyman kisses the King and Prince Selim and Prince Bayezit do the same. The Sultan doesn't care for the boy's given name and in this way Stephen, who cannot fail to grow up a Hungarian patriot, becomes John Sigismund, who might be anyone.

While the delegation is in the Ottoman camp, the Janissaries wander into the city, one by one, as if by chance and out of curiosity. Employing a softer, more subtle version of the stratagem that was used at Diu, they take possession of the gates and other strategic locations while criers announce that property rights will be respected provided the people give up their arms. And before the people of Buda know what has happened, the city is Ottoman.

In due course the boy is returned to his mother but Brother George and the others are detained in the Turkish camp, and if there's one thing worse than having councillors who wish to dominate you on account of your sex, youth and foreignness, it's having no councillors at all.

The Governor of Belgrade advises the Sultan to take a hard line: put the councillors to the sword and pack John Sigismund off to Istanbul while sending Isabella back to Poland. As for the kingdom at large, 'let their barons be killed and their fortresses levelled, and from every region let those families that show the most spirit be exiled to Asia while the rest of the multitude who work the fields and inhabit the cities be suppressed by the placing of garrisons, for only then . . . will they know themselves to be tamed.'

Isabella is not the airhead they say she is and she understands that the people whose sympathy she needs are not the men across the river but the women in Istanbul. Hurrem and

Mihrimah feel for their royal sister who must cope with widow-hood, motherhood and all those boring sieges far from home and quite alone. Not that their sympathy for embattled members of their own sex is indiscriminate. It does not extend to Mahidevran. But Isabella is poor and beautiful and her father is the King of Poland. The Sultan's wife and daughter would be appalled if the Governor of Belgrade's cruel proposals were put into effect. They would give their husbands hell.

While her future is being debated Isabella courts Mihrimah through her husband, sending affectionate notes across the river along with gifts that include a necklace of pearls with a pendant of jewels. And Rustem advises Suleyman that for a great prince there is no surer path to infamy than to break a promise that was made to a woman and a child.

On 3 September Isabella receives a diploma in which the Sultan confirms in letters of azure and gold that John Sigismund will assume the functions of the King of Hungary when he attains his majority. The boy is also sent a standard which signifies that in the meantime he is to be Governor of the semi-detached principality of Transylvania. On 6 September Isabella, John Sigismund and Brother George are escorted out of the city and in a south-easterly direction towards their new home.

After the Queen's departure Nicholas von Salm returns with another ambassador, Sigismund von Herberstein. Put up an arrow's shot from Rustem's tent and regaled with delicacies of the field and the vine, he delivers yet another of Ferdinand's unavailing demands that the Sultan hand over Hungary in return for an annual tribute. An incredulous Rustem demands, 'do you think that [the Sultan] is so foolish as to give up that which he has won with the sword for the third time?' He is referring to the two previous occasions when Suleyman took Buda but failed to incorporate it into the Empire, an omission that has now been put right.

The following day the Austrians are received by the Sultan according to protocol, that is to say, with a man gripping an arm on either side and giving every appearance of doing the visitor an honour while in fact preventing him from withdrawing a dagger or raising a fist.

Back in 1532 a Hapsburg embassy tried to dissuade Suleyman from invading Austria by offering him such cheap gifts, jugs and vases dipped in a little bit of gold, that the Sultan laid waste to the Austrian valleys with redoubled vigour. That lesson has been learned. While the Sultan sits on an ornate bed under a gold baldachin, a dozen of the ambassadors' servants carry in an enormous silver clock. This object of splendid wonder, which shows not only the passage of the hours but also the motion of the stars, the conjunctions of the planets and the solar and lunar months, belonged to the Emperor Maximilian, Charles and Ferdinand's late father. And the Ottoman Sultan, whose courtesy titles include 'Master of the Celestial Conjunction' and is the ideal recipient of such a gift, observes with undisguised pleasure as the horologist snaps open the clock's buckles exposing wheels with teeth and weights and counterweights, which operate in accordance with the supreme or divine motor who orders time itself. The technician also hands over instructions explaining what to do if the clock breaks down.

Before he quits Buda the Sultan receives Francis's new envoy, Captain Polin, so called because he is a man of war, and together they deplore the discovery of Rincon and Fregoso's mangled bodies in Milanese territory. The plan now, Polin explains, is for the Most Christian King to burst out of France to attack Charles on several fronts, if the Sultan will be so good as to send Barbarossa to the northern Mediterranean in concert with the French fleet. Next year, the Sultan replies soothingly, or failing that the year after. And when he gets home he is gratified to learn that the Emperor has got his feet wet.

∼

A city of between three and four thousand hearths, an entrepot of Christian slaves, leather and copper goods, silk belts, embroidered handkerchiefs, cotton, dates and honey, Algiers is built up the slope of a mountain, its walls converging at its highest point which is crowned by a fort identifiable from the lime with which it is coated. Inside the town the buildings of private individuals, receding little by little from the flattest street above the sea-shore, stretch up the mountainside as if by degrees and there is no house from which one cannot see all the others.

Hayreddin Barbarossa's elder brother Oruc captured the town from the Spanish in 1516. Then Oruc was killed and Hayreddin completed the conquest by expelling the Spanish from a stronghold they had established on a rock at the mouth of the bay. Now Algiers is governed by Hayreddin's eunuch protégé Hassan.

Hassan started life as a shepherd in Sardinia. 'While being slight of stature,' Murat the chronicler writes, 'when it came to his heart and his valour and courage [Hassan] was a very big person,' and beloved of the people of Algiers where 'everyone lives with contentment and gratitude.'

Less beloved of the Spanish, for, as Murat continues, Hassan 'acquired thirty galleys and galliots and every day they come to the Spanish lands and continuously pillage the towers and fortresses on the coasts and won't let the [Spanish] ships sail on the seas . . . and for this reason whenever the King of Spain wishes to sail his fleet [from Spain] to Greece he makes sure it is known . . . that Algiers is occupied by the lowliest slave of Barbarossa who is in the nature of a woman.'

Even Charles's friends don't share his view that the autumn of 1541 is the time for a foreign adventure. What is the justification, Pope Paul asks, for attacking a distant pinprick when Buda is falling to the Turks? And Doria observes in his sailorly fashion that in winter the coast of North Africa is 'extremely stormy . . . if we go there, we will all perish,' to which Charles replies with his emperor's belly-laugh, 'twenty-two years of empire for me, and seventy-two years of life for you, should suffice for us to die content!'

There's no deflecting a man who when he doesn't get his way is liable to hold his head in his hands and sulk for six hours before reappearing looking unutterably sad. So Paul reluctantly blesses the enterprise, Doria weighs anchor and on 19 October, having witnessed, at Sardinia, the unsettling augury of a calf born with two heads, the Emperor reaches the bay of Algiers. His force is composed of twenty-three thousand footsoldiers, three thousand volunteers of various nations, four hundred knights of Malta and several thousand mariners. His five hundred and sixteen vessels carry heavy guns, horses, cows, sheep, one hundred and fifty thousand ducats harvested from the Peruvian mines and a contingent of Spanish ladies dressed as if for a tournament.

Charles's personnel include his high steward the Duke of Alba, Ferrante Gonzaga, Viceroy of Sicily, who has recently purchased a countship on the banks of the Po, and Hernan Cortes, fresh from the Baja California peninsula and boasting that he has won for the Emperor more provinces in the New World than his forebears left him cities in the old. And these gentlemen, who travel anything but light, with valets and changes of clothes, chests of treasure, crucifixes and horses, execrate the eunuch herdsman who stands against them.

On 23 October the army disembarks and a knight called Lorenzo Manuel approaches the city with a white flag attached to his pikestaff. The meeting takes place in a room with a high vault lighted by a lamp taken from a Spanish church. Manuel asks: are you not a Sardinian turned by compulsion from the religion of your birth and is the power you currently enjoy not the gift of a usurper? And he passes on the Emperor's advice that Hassan should surrender Algiers and 'like a bird save yourself from my hand or I will have all the stones of your castle thrown into the sea and . . . destroy and devastate your lands.'

Hassan is one of those eunuchs whose beauty stops you in your tracks. His answer to the Emperor is crystalline. 'You are a dog who pretends to be a king,' he says, 'and your business is blood and deceit.' Hassan vows to ensure that 'the disgraceful fleet of the death-meriting infidels meets the fate it deserves,' and he recalls that an earlier Spanish expedition to recapture Algiers ended in disaster, saying, 'thanks be to God fleets that have come to this place have not left and you will suffer the same only worse.'

That night the Christians build trenches and Hassan and his men come out of the city and fall on them with cries of 'Allah! Allah!' But the defenders are outnumbered ten to one and they can do little to stop the Emperor deploying his forces, until, at nine o'clock on the evening of 24 October, the huge army is in position under the city walls. It is now that the storm begins and, in the words of a participant, 'there wasn't a soldier who in the space of a single moment wasn't as wet as if he had been dropped into the sea.'

~

Charles was perhaps thinking of Tunis where the problem wasn't water but its lack; where only the wells of Carthage saved the army from dying of thirst. But that was June and this is October when the northerlies scream across the Mediterranean bearing gifts.

Anticipating a quick victory he sent his men ashore without tents and with provisions for just two days. Accommodation and food will be found in abundance in the fallen city. So ran his thinking until 9 pm on 24 October.

Within a few hours the storm renders a modern army totally ineffective. The powder is putty, the match won't light. Where are the crossbows? Left behind in the age of chivalry. Where are the trees to try and burn for warmth? Hassan cut them down. In the words of Nicolas Durand de Villegaignon, a commander of the knights of Malta, 'the enemy came out in large numbers to occupy our positions, leaping into our lines, and killed us with arrows in prodigious numbers, the rain and the wind striking our faces. We nonetheless took up our arms but the enemy withdrew ... and in our pursuit we fell into their ambushes.'

Sodden and battered, the Christians stagger to false refuges: to gullies that are torrents and spurs that are mudslides. As for those troops who are closest to the city, 'at the foot of the wall,' as the saying goes, 'but without a ladder,' the defenders kill them using crossbow bolts, darts, javelins, rocks, masonry and every kind of lethal projectile. Hassan himself leads mounted squadrons that come out of the city and launch lightning attacks before streaking back inside the walls again.

Back to the ships! If only that were possible. Many vessels, writes Villegaignon, 'could no longer endure the cruelty of the sea, their anchor ropes were severed, some of them pitched onto the land while others filled with water and sank with many hands and beasts, lost and drowned, which calamity was greatly augmented at the break of day when the wind and rain grew to such a great rage that almost no one could stand on his feet.' Meanwhile the enemy 'assembled in large numbers on the beach the better to kill those unfortunate enough to be tossed ashore'.

The sense of isolation at the heart of every melee, the snap of spines when riders are thrown, the weariness of footsoldiers carrying their weight in water. As the Emperor's Italian troops flee they are confronted by their master who asks how they hope to find salvation at sea if they lose purchase on land. Only the knights of Malta are steadfast, they and a handful of valiant Italians who, ashamed at the cowardice of their compatriots, gather under the Maltese Cross. When the knights are surrounded by enemy horsemen smiting them with axes and hurling javelins with uncanny accuracy at the joints of their armour, the Emperor himself comes to their aid and taking his place in the first rank shows no fear or surprise when the men either side of him fall dead.

The army's wheat, flour, biscuit, peas, beans, wine, oil and salt meat are on the sea floor and the men are so famished they eat palm roots. The next day, 25 October, Charles gives the order for the horses to be killed for food. He starts with his own and as an encouragement to his men declares it delicious.

Doria stands offshore, firing from his galley, the *Temperance*, in support of the land forces. And it's no accident that the sunken ships are mostly Spanish and not under Doria's command. They were anchored with a single anchor while Doria gave orders for his Genoese vessels to be anchored using two.

After some days he sends a strong swimmer ashore with a message for the Emperor that the sea is somewhat calmed.

Between 31 October and 2 November the surviving men are taken off the shore under heavy rain and enemy harassment. The munitions and remaining horses and other items not bolted down are tipped overboard to make room. Some fourteen hundred slaves flee in the opposite direction, abandoning the oar bench for the warm embrace of their fellow Muslims. Eighteen thousand Christians are left for dead and of the four thousand horses that were brought on the expedition it is said that all were killed by the Muslims, eaten by the Christians or thrown into the sea to give space to evacuees.

Approaching the ship that is to take him away, Charles must ford a river that breaks its banks as it flows into the sea, causing him to lose his footing. Only a Muslim guide, placing himself in the middle of the torrent, saves the Emperor from drowning. Putting in further up the coast he leads prayers for better weather until, on 23 November, the gale abates and he sails away with the remains of the armada.

Arriving back in Genoa Andrea Doria holds a solemn Mass before going home and locking the door. Not that a locked door is a bar to misfortune. That winter the *Temperance* is accidentally blown up while at anchor and Doria's wife leaves him, taking the good furniture.

'The Emperor,' runs a French report, 'will remember for the rest of his life the enormous loss he has just suffered.' For some months afterwards Charles's guards must travel around Spain by mule because so many horses were lost. Along the coast of North Africa people pick their way among debris retrieving shiny buckles and gem-studded swords, damp silks in smashed chests and a canteen of silver plate that the English ambassador, who was rescued from the maelstrom in just his shirt, intended to feature in a programme of hospitality following the city's liberation.

Act Three: The Sea, the Strait and the Horn

IX

Preachers abound in our day and age. The Porte's present prig is the Grand Vizier, Lutfi Pasha. Whoever occupies this noble office, he tells anyone who'll listen, 'must do all for God, in the path of God and for the satisfaction of God. For there is no higher station that can be attained.' Quite. Here is another of his aphorisms. 'It is a great ill and a pain without remedy for a statesman to take a bribe.' This from a man who accepted a globe worth one hundred and fifty thousand crowns from Antonio Rincon.

He's the kind of blockhead who, when presented with a laboriously translated Turkish version of the *Panchatantra*, an anthology of Indian fables of great antiquity and wisdom, asks the translator if he wouldn't have been better off spending the past twenty years dealing with some questions of the law.

Even Lutfi's friends wouldn't claim that he has the verve of an Ibrahim or the shrewdness of a Rustem. This perhaps explains why Suleyman promoted him in the first place. The festivities he organised in 1539 when the Sultan's younger sons were circumcised were a week shorter than those staged by Ibrahim for the elder princes nine years earlier. Lutfi considered this a feat of thrift. To others it was a false economy. What is the point of such events if not to dazzle the world?

Tight with money, generous with mud, especially if it lands on dead predecessors. Expatiating on the qualities that are required in a grand vizier, he says that the job shouldn't go to anyone who is 'obsessed with fornication'. This is a swipe at Ayas Pasha and his forty cots. 'Music-lovers and drinkers' shouldn't be considered either. Remember Ibrahim the Frank? Naturally he doesn't approve of assertive females and he and Hurrem don't see eye to eye.

One may wonder what it is like to be married to such a desiccated and savourless person. Suleyman's sister Sah Sultan has had the pleasure these past years though her devotion is increasingly directed at a charismatic sheikh called Merkez Efendi. The inventor of a celebrated paste with occult qualities, Merkez Efendi was attached to the pious foundation that Hafsa endowed in Manisa when young Suleyman was Governor there. Mother and son developed a fondness for the sheikh whose sermons made the Prince weep. Later on Merkez Efendi was appointed army sheikh on the Corfu campaign of 1537, which was led by Lutfi Pasha, Sah Sultan travelling in her husband's retinue. On the way back to Istanbul Sah Sultan's wagon was attacked by bandits but a miraculous intervention by Merkez Efendi saved her life.

Whether it's Sah Sultan's infatuation with the sheikh or the unseemly joy that comes over her husband when he discovers that the household accounts are in surplus, there have long been grounds for marital tension. Then in the summer of 1541 a sin of the flesh is brought to Lutfi's attention and his complacency and lack of imagination react catastrophically with the bigot inside.

Prostitutes are far from rare in this city of ours. If you duck round the back of Hurrem's foundation or into the recesses of the Hippodrome, you won't be alone for long. On this occasion the discovery of a prostitute about her trade so offends the Grand Vizier that he has her genitals cut with a razor.

'How could you devise so cruel a torture?' Sah Sultan demands when she hears what he has done. But Lutfi only accepts scoldings from God. 'The punishment suits the crime!' he shoots back, adding that the same sanction will henceforth be applied to 'all women who dishonour themselves in the eyes of religion and the law'.

'Barbarian! Tyrant!' screams his wife. Every marriage has a breaking point. Lutfi leaps on her raining blows and pulling her hair. Alerted by the commotion, the ladies-in-waiting and eunuchs come running, drag the Grand Vizier off the Sultan's sister and expel him with punches and howls. And Sah Sultan takes a carriage to her brother to demand a divorce.

~

When Lutfi arrives at the Second Court for the next meeting of the Imperial Council, the doorkeeper bars his way and asks if he wishes to separate from his wife, to which he answers, no, he does not. Had he said yes, the Sultan would have cut off his head. An Albanian slave has no place petitioning for divorce from the Sultan's sister.

It is interesting to consider how often Suleyman is on the verge of executing someone, only to relent. He's the kind of sultan who starts angry then softens. His father would start angry then harden. Not that Lutfi shows any sign of realising how lucky he is to live under Suleyman and not Selim. After accomplishing the pilgrimage to Mecca the former vizier is allowed to retire to Dimetoka, cushioned by his ex-wife's dowry of one hundred thousand ducats and his own impregnable self-regard.

Under the divorce settlement Sah Sultan gets the palace but when she returns to the scene of that dreadful episode she passes out and has to be carried to bed on a carpet. She is also awarded some of Lutfi's properties in town which her brother tops up with villages that will bring in an income. One advantage of her split from Lutfi, other than the obvious one, is that she will be able to devote more time and money to building mosques, lodges and other foundations for Sheikh Merkez.

Lutfi's departure from the Imperial Council removes a powerful supporter of Prince Mustafa from the scene. No longer is there any obstacle to the Prince's transfer from the conveniently nearby governorship of Manisa to the disadvantageously distant one of Amasya. This setback for the Sultan's eldest son is camouflaged by an increase in his stipend and an enlarged troop of Janissaries. But exile is exile, no matter how you spin it. In 1542 Prince Mehmet is appointed to the governorship of Manisa and Prince Selim to that of Karaman, with his court in the city of Konya. When the time comes Mustafa's younger half-brothers will both enjoy a geographical advantage over him.

After Lutfi's disgrace the staggeringly ancient Hadim Suleyman is elevated, or perhaps winched, to the Grand Vizierate and a nonentity rises to Second. Rustem goes to Third but everyone knows that he is more powerful than his position in the pecking order suggests. It is he who lives with the Sultan's daughter a stone's throw from the New Palace. It is he who calls the Sultan's wife mother.

A troika or cabal of the Sultan's nearest and dearest is coming into being, one that sits on his shoulder and tells him what to do, a cabal whose aim is to put Rustem into the Grand Vizierate, Prince Mehmet into the New Palace and Prince Mustafa into the ground.

And Hurrem has stumbled on an excellent formula for acquiring a grand vizier. Marry your daughter to the Fourth Vizier and wait.

X

The moneylenders of Venice have learned not to advance cash to an agent of the King of France. It is liable to go astray. But Captain Polin in Constantinople needs money to do the King's work and a banker comes forward with a cache of coins that were struck during the occupation of France by Henry V of England more than a century ago. A courier takes the coins from Venice to Dalmatia only to disappear without trace and when specie of this description turns up in the local markets it is clear that the courier fell foul of scoundrels of the kind that did for Rincon.

Captain Polin is Rincon without the love handles. It takes him just twenty-one days to travel from Constantinople to see Francis a continent away. After one such journey he entertains the court at Fontainebleau with his description of the large panache of phoenix feathers that the Sultan was wearing when he last saw him, not that all are convinced, it being common knowledge that there is only one phoenix in the whole world which will combust when it is time to die, to which Polin replies that the phoenix drops feathers like any other bird and the Sultan's zeal as a collector explains his possession of such a panache, adding that 'nothing stands in the way of the curiosity of such a great lord, for with a blink of his eye his wishes are carried out with exactitude.'

When Polin's money isn't being stolen the Frenchman buys

outcomes in Istanbul using gifts. To the Sultan he presents a huge canteen of silver goods and to the Pashas, the officers of the New Palace and the porters five hundred robes of silk and other rich cloth. And if his secret route is made public he wrong-foots would-be assassins by boarding the regular service across the Adriatic like any ordinary merchant or pilgrim.

~

In the summer of 1543 Francis opens fronts against Charles in Roussillon, in south-western France, and in Luxemburg on his north-eastern frontier. The following May the Sultan marches against the Hungarian fortresses that Ferdinand seized two years ago. He also orders Hayreddin to France's Mediterranean coast with a fleet of one hundred and ten galleys and huge transports that were captured in the defeat of the Holy League at Prevesa. The Captain Pasha's orders, Suleyman informs Francis in a letter, are 'to follow your instructions and to compass his actions to the ruin of your enemies'. Not that the Sultan harbours any illusions about his ally's reliability, warning him to 'take care that your enemy does not dupe you; only when he recognises that you have sufficient resolve to make continuous war against him will he be reduced to making peace.'

It's one thing for the French and Turks to fool around in the warm waters of the Adriatic and Ionian Seas, another for a huge Muslim armada to be ushered northwards, ever northwards, by the eldest daughter of the Church of Rome! Captain Polin is to accompany Barbarossa in his new capacity as Lieutenant-General of France's Levantine fleet, which comes with a flagship, four more vessels flying French colours, and a title, Baron de La Garde. Polin's trepidation as the combined fleet sets out is that of a minder escorting a bride who brings a big dowry but is sure to misbehave.

At Reggio in Calabria on the way north the Hapsburg Governor, Diego Gaetano, kills three Turks: Hayreddin's prompt to enter the town, burn it and enslave the survivors. His salty old lubricious eye falls on the Governor's daughter Maria. A lesson in the rudiments of Islam, a halting attestation of the faith, and the pirate king has his queen.

On 29 June the armada drops anchor in the mouth of the Tiber. A day away in Rome terrified citizens stampede to the house of the Papal Legate, Paul himself having left town to consult with the Emperor on the Lutheran question, and that night soldiers have to be sent with torches to stop citizens fleeing for the hills, matrons in particular, while nuns from local monasteries run about weeping and caring nothing for their name or honour. 'Captain Polin,' one Roman drolly observes, 'has given us to understand that there is no cause for alarm, because the Grand Turk has expressly ordered Barbarossa not to molest the Pope's lands. There's a religious scruple which was not suspected . . . perhaps that prophecy will be fulfilled which says that he will become a Christian!'

The welcome salute with which the Count of Enghien, Lieutenant-General of Francis's Provence fleet, greets the Turkish armada when it arrives at Marseille on 20 July lacks nothing in noise, the feast he hosts in Barbarossa's honour also being very splendid with a band playing melodies that are pleasing to Turkish ears as well as French ones. But Barbarossa is irritated by the lack of provisions for his men, the lack of a campaign plan, the typically French unpreparedness, and he tells Polin to fetch orders and be quick about it or he will face Turkish displeasure.

In the Low Countries Polin finds the Most Christian King with his army around him and Charles not far away with his. Francis is taken aback to learn that the Ottoman fleet stands a little menacingly off his southern shore. He perhaps mistook the Sultan's word of honour for his own. And back goes Polin at top speed with goodies for Hayreddin: silver plate, a sword, an objective.

~

The town of Nice is in Hapsburg hands. It sits next to a high mountain with a fortress on top and descends to the sea in a continuous slope. Bastions were recently added by the constable,

Paolo Simeoni, a knight of Malta who eight years ago was in Barbarossa's prison at Tunis and had the honour of leading a revolt of Christian slaves there. Simeoni has such a poor opinion of his former gaoler that he hangs Barbarossa's messenger who arrives to accept his surrender.

Is this a first, Catholics assaulting other Catholics using superior Muslim firepower? Barbarossa speedily disembarks his cannons and digs trenches before launching a bombardment of such accuracy that the balls strike the very crowns of the ramparts, all the while receiving indifferent help from his French friends whose ordnance sails wide of the target and into the Turkish camp. And so destructive is the Turkish cannonade, the mortar holding the bastions being not quite dry, that they soon topple and the people of Nice shout their wish to surrender to which Enghien replies with promises of clemency and good treatment.

No. Hayreddin Barbarossa hasn't sailed three thousand miles to dispense clemency and good treatment. Clemency and good treatment are for people who surrender at the first time of asking, not people who kill and maim up to one hundred Turks, as the defenders of Nice have done. Enter Captain Polin who needs all his diplomacy to persuade Barbarossa to stop the Janissaries looting the town of Nice and all his agility to avoid being murdered when they find out what he has cost them.

Simeoni retreats to the fortress but no sooner do the Turks and French direct their guns in its direction than Polin comes to Barbarossa saying he has run out of powder and ball and would His Excellency mind giving him some?

Age frees the tongue. And Barbarossa, who doesn't need to draw himself up or puff himself out, being a great grizzled sexed-up bugaboo, gives his frank opinion of his allies who are so unserious they fill their holds with wine rather than cannon balls and so disrespectful they trifle with his honour and put him to expense. Then he convenes his captains and Janissaries and they decide, with the unanimity of swallows, to fly south.

Again it falls to the Baron de la Garde, this man with a small fleet and a big name, to dissuade the Turks from a departure that would expose the whole southern coast of France to Hapsburg attack. Addressing the Janissaries who tried to murder him, he regrets that if they go away they will miss out on the famed generosity of the King of France. He notes that the Sultan might be less than pleased to hear that the Captain Pasha has abandoned his brother monarch in a time of need. And the swallows reconsider.

War is weather. Andrea Doria and the Marquis of Vasto arrive to save Nice for the Emperor but a storm rises and the Marquis's ship is only saved from breaking on the rocks by a quick-thinking seaman who raises the foresail and brings her about. Doria's galleys are less fortunate, four of them being shattered by a steepling cascade of water, with no time to unchain the rowers who are pulled gurgling to the bottom.

On 8 September the siege of Nice is lifted. The Turkish gunners are so brawny that they carry their cannons on their backs and amaze the French gunners by carrying theirs too. Barbarossa withdraws to Antibes, a short distance down the coast, but Polin sends an envoy racing after him, a poet who speaks to the pirate king in Greek, the language of his youth back in Lesbos, and informs him that Doria's crippled ships have limped into the open sea, their masts snapped and their sails in tatters, and that now, if ever there was a time, is the time to kill off Andrea Doria. But Polin doesn't understand the relationship between the two men.

More than Maria Gaetano will ever be, it is Doria who is Barbarossa's spouse of long standing. And Barbarossa says let us wait for the storm to abate and then tarries outrageously beneath the vines of Antibes, which greatly amuses his captains who joke that mutually assured preservation is the doctrine of pirates. A greenhorn in Hayreddin's company criticises the Pasha's slowness, to which he replies tolerantly that he, an old captain, sees things with his eyes shut which a young man does not see with his eyes open.

The end of the fighting season is logged in the Ottoman

campaign record: 'And the brilliance of the flags of the victorious ships . . . whose cannons have razed the coast, the forts and the citadels of France like lightning; as well as the sparkle of the lances, similar to shooting stars, of the triumphant soldiers shedding the blood of traitors, had turned the surface of the water into a rose garden. The ships themselves had become like fields of tulips . . . and this splendour exalted the sea and spread agitation among the fish it accommodates. And it was in such a way that the valiant Pasha came and dropped anchor before the fine town of Toulon.'

~

The Most Christian King insists that what the world knows as his alliance with the Turks is in fact 'a truce or a suspension of warfare from which no Christian state is excluded'. He dismisses claims that letters were found on Rincon in which he, Francis, asked the Turk to come against the Christians. But it's not a good look when the bay of Toulon is invisible for ships flying the crescent of Islam.

The lieutenant of Provence has received instructions to 'lodge the Lord Barbarossa sent to the king by the Great Turk, with his Turkish army and great lords to the number of thirty thousand combatants during the winter'. In addition he is advised that 'it will not be suitable for the inhabitants of Toulon to remain and mingle with the Turkish nation because of difficulties which might arise.' And so this port city made up of houses with sloping tiled roofs behind high walls and towers, but now without artillery on the ramparts, the guns having been removed by the authorities lest their guests misuse them, is emptied of five thousand souls.

When Barbarossa's men enter the town there are none of the harsh oaths and discordant trumpet blasts that are a regrettable feature of Christian navies, but each man is soberly intent on his task, the captains with their slaves occupying the best houses and the men pitching their tents beyond the city walls. Tall trees are felled for masts and the mulberry crop is dried on mats in the Turkish manner. Hearing the call to prayer issue from the cathedral, seat of the bishops of Toulon these past one thousand years, a French observer murmurs, 'one would think one at Constantinople . . .'

The author of the Ottoman campaign record is evidently on retainer from the Toulon tourist board. 'The weather is very temperate,' he writes, 'and a cooling wind blows without interruption. In spring the town flourishes and all the fields are full of flowers . . . innumerable bloom the flowers on each of its trees. When its rose garden is in bloom the plaints of the nightingale fill the ear. Without equal in the lands of the Franks, this place bewitches whoever beholds it.' Yes, there are worse places for the Captain Pasha and his lady to kick off their slippers and get acquainted.

And to judge by the receipts that are passed on to the Treasury of France, the honeymooners take their downtime seriously. In quick succession bills are raised for lambs, kids, a dray with a capacity of four or five jars of good white or red wine, five hundred pomegranates, four rabbits, some brace of partridge, hens, eight hundred prized calville apples from the orchard of Antoine Gaubert, three hundred sour oranges, many quarts of olive oil, two hundred pears on the occasion of St Andrew's Day, more lambs . . .

Only the pigs are safe.

In November the councillors of Toulon express their concern to Captain Polin regarding 'the widespread panic currently affecting the Toulon region, stemming from the stripping day by day of the olive trees by foreigners and their other depredations,' also drawing his attention to 'the poverty that afflicts the . . . tenant farmers who . . . following the King's orders, in lodging the Turks in their houses, are obliged to live elsewhere enduring many travails'.

Having stored many examples of French treachery in his heart, Hayreddin seems determined to enjoy his revenge. When he submits his demand for ship's biscuit to his French hosts he doesn't confine himself to his present and future needs but includes all the biscuit that his armada consumed while sailing north this past summer, a full five months of raiding, which comes to eighty-seven thousand quintals. Taking into account the requirements of his land troops and a flotilla he sends to pester northern Spain, his total demand comes to the almost incomprehensibly large sum of two hundred thousand quintals.

Well might the lieutenant of Provence sigh that Barbarossa 'takes his ease while emptying the coffers of France'.

Pity Captain Polin in the winter of 1543–4. Whether he is extracting an advance from a Lyonnais alderman to help him defray his Turkish expenses or freeing Provencal peasants who have been enslaved by rogue Janissaries, his sole and overriding objective is to survive the unspeakable house guest that is Hayreddin Barbarossa.

On Francis's orders he keeps the pirate king under constant surveillance, particularly his dealings with Doria, ruler of Genoa, and sure enough that winter Hayreddin buys the freedom of one of his most brilliant captains, Turgut, for the suspiciously low sum of three thousand ducats, also granting his Genoese friends a licence to harvest coral off the coast of North Africa.

Forget the examples of French double-dealing that the Emperor presented to his audience in the Papal robing chamber a few years ago; the welcome that Francis has afforded Barbarossa in Toulon gives new meaning to the word 'betrayal'. In February 1544 the French delegate to an imperial diet is prevented from attending on the grounds that his master is 'as much an enemy of Christendom as the Turk himself'. And on Lake Como that observer of broad and balanced perspective, Paolo Giovio, is moved to wonder why the Most Christian King 'had to leave the Christian nations prey to the cruel barbarians, a fate they in no way deserve, simply because they followed the empire of the Emperor? Why in such a cruel act must he forget his ancient nickname? And why, ultimately, did he have to leave behind a hateful memory of himself?'

~

In the spring of 1544 thirty French Treasury officials arrive in Toulon and over three days and three nights they fill sacks of money totalling eight hundred thousand ecus which they hand over to Barbarossa. After ransacking five French galleys and freeing all Muslim slaves in the French fleet, Barbarossa sets out for home with unfinished business to attend to en route, and he insists that Polin accompany him with his five ships.

Approaching Elba, Hayreddin writes to the lord of that island, saying, 'I know you have had for a long time among your slaves a young Turk who was taken at Tunis, son of the general of the galleys, Sinan, known as "the Jew". I would like you very lovingly to return him to me.'

Sinan the Jew is as good a seaman as Hayreddin and as stern a master but less moody. In fact he isn't Jewish but his knowledge of the stars is close to rabbinical. He's at Suez building a fresh fleet to launch another invasion of India and there's a hole the shape of his son where his heart should be.

The lord of Elba replies to Hayreddin saying that since the boy has been baptised into the Christian faith and cannot be returned without sin he hopes that the Captain Pasha will be content with a selection of premium produce from the island.

In fact Hayreddin is content to land his men and occupy the olive terraces and enslave the islanders who try to flee over thorny crags and through woods, and his contentment brings the lord of Elba to his senses. Sinan's son is returned and the Captain Pasha embraces him, gives him seven galleys and points him towards Suez.

Next up is Talamone, a promontory on the Tuscan mainland. Hayreddin's pupil Salah and his sixty ships land to take slaves. Then Barbarossa turns his prows towards the castle and bombards it. Coming ashore he makes for the house of Bartholomew, the recently deceased Captain of the Pope's galleys, burning it and destroying Bartholomew's tomb and chucking about his bones. This is to pay back Bartholomew for plundering Barbarossa's ancestral home of Lesbos and damaging his lands there.

Further south, the town of Porto Ercole is served by two harbours and rises to a well-watered plateau dressed in olive trees, palms and myrtles, an ideal place to build a great city should any of today's kings possess the same hunger for glory as did the ancient Greeks and Romans before them. Sultan Suleyman, in other words, who is on the lookout for a bridgehead from which to conquer Italy.

But the Captain Pasha has been shipwrecked twice in his career, with the loss of many galleys, and the prudent navigator in him knows that he must press on if he is to avoid being crushed by the doubtful storms of uncertain autumn. He stays just long enough to lay waste to Ercole and to receive Diego Gaetano who kisses Maria fondly and is treated by Barbarossa with all the honour and affection due a father-in-law.

All the while the French are . . . the French. Polin knows that if Barbarossa does not get home well satisfied and laden with booty, he, Polin, risks becoming another Laski. The more damage is done to these Hapsburg lands, the weaker Charles's position will be at the peace talks that recently opened between his and Francis's representatives. So while Barbarossa retraces Charles's northward progress of '35, substituting fire, fetters and screams for imperial smiles, Polin and his French passengers, who include adventurers and men of the cloth, avert their gaze from the distressing scenes to which they are exposed.

~

During a stop-over at Policastro, south of Naples, Barbarossa intercepts a local man who is kind enough to bring Polin a gift and enslaves the man without any justification, upon which Polin, 'being a very wise man, pretended he knew nothing of this, governing himself according to circumstance'.

So writes Jerome Maurand, priest of Antibes, who is Polin's almoner, or distributor of alms. Maurand has long desired to see Constantinople and he yearns especially to stand beneath the dome of Aya Sofya. On the voyage south he distracts himself with excursions to admire ruins and taste local delicacies, for instance, the species of grape that is peculiar to the Aeolian island of Salina and produces delicious raisins.

On 2 July, on the island of Volcano, in the same archipelago, he comes ashore and picks his way up a steep slope, as he writes, 'with great difficulty as this mountain is composed of congealed ash formed into channels and pits'. Eventually attaining a summit from which 'smoke was emanating, and seeing such a horrible and deep cavern, vomiting fire and smoke and giving off an intolerable and very strong smell of sulphur,' he is reminded of the chasm of Tartarus where the wicked receive punishment. From the locals Maurand learns that the last time the mountain erupted, burning forests on the neighbouring island of Lipari, the women of the latter promised God that if the fire stopped short of their town of two thousand homes they would cease drinking alcohol and walk barefoot in recognition of his clemency. Which is exactly what happened.

That same day Hayreddin lands five and a half thousand men and sixteen cannons on Lipari. Then he begins a bombardment of the fortress in the course of which three notables come out and offer him fifteen thousand ducats in return for leaving the island alone. Hayreddin's counter-demand is thirty thousand ducats in addition to two hundred little girls and two hundred little boys, adding that if his conditions are not met he will burn the town and destroy the region. Convinced more than ever that Barbarossa intends to wage war rather than make peace, the notables return to the fortress and the bombardment intensifies.

On 7 July some men are caught escaping from the fortress and tell the Pasha that the people inside are divided over whether or not to carry on resisting. In the early hours of 9 July, Giannettino Doria, Andrea Doria's younger cousin and second-in-command, approaches Lipari with some galleys but is put to flight by Polin. On the ninth day of the bombardment, four men come out and offer to surrender the city with the exception of seventy houses, their inhabitants and contents, and the Pasha consents. But those Lipariotes not lucky enough to live in one of the seventy houses block the plan and insist that everyone must go into captivity or no one at all.

By the time Lipari falls without prior agreement the Turkish cannons have fired a total of two thousand eight hundred rounds and the walls are in ruins. The people are paraded before the Pasha who personally strikes down the decrepit and enslaves the fit. A group of Turks enter a church where some very old people are hiding and they cut them open while they are still alive, in order, they say, to take their gall bladders, for gall has many useful qualities.

In this way the town of Lipari is reduced and its able-bodied population of nine thousand people, men and women, boys and girls, are chained and put onto Turkish ships. In the absence of their human overlords the raddled curs of the island turn into ferocious wolves and hunt down the sheep on the hillsides. That afternoon Lipari is burned to the ground and a further one thousand people who had evaded the Turks by hiding in cellars and caves are forced out by the flames and into captivity.

By now the morally alive observer is in a kind of stupor, oppressed by a sense that the will of God has not been fully divulged for there must be a reason for the tragedy of Lipari.

No, God isn't easy to read but Jerome Maurand will have a go. And when he asks himself why the people of Lipari have been selected for such atrocious torments and why Barbarossa succeeded in burning the town when the vomiting mountain failed, his answer is simple.

'In his wrath,' Maurand writes, '[God] sends . . . plagues onto the Church which is a veritable Babylon, and not really Christian, to avenge himself on his enemies with the help of his [other] enemies. And I say that because, as I was told by a person . . . who had lived at Lipari and married a woman of Lipari . . . these Lipariotes were very fond of the sin of sodomy, so much so that when they saw a handsome young man, in order to enjoy that young man they would consent for him to lie with their wives, even in the presence of the husband.' Nowhere in Maurand's analysis does he make room for the complicity and collusion of the perfidious, hypocritical, pharisaical French.

On September 18 representatives of King Francis and of the Hapsburgs sign an accord at Crepy in northern France. Under the accords, Francis's son Charles of Orleans is to marry either the Emperor's eldest daughter, the Infanta Maria, with a dowry consisting of the Netherlands and Franche-Comté, or one of Ferdinand's daughters, whose dowry will be the Duchy of Milan. The Emperor has four months to decide which. For his part Francis undertakes to fight the Turks and to help suppress Lutheranism in Germany.

In view of the the King's alliance with his brother Suleyman, his relaxed attitude towards words like 'undertake', 'pledge' and 'promise', and the Emperor's attachment to Milan and the Netherlands, it remains to be seen which provisions of Crepy, if any, will come to pass. But no war lasts forever.

~

After sailing past the Princes' Islands one approaches the battlemented walls that encircle Constantinople in an unbroken line. Behind lies the Propontis or Sea of Marmara, antechamber of the Mediterranean, and ahead the Bosporus, a broad strait leading to the Black Sea whose perverse and attested attribute is that it flows in two directions at once. To the right Asia ascends without drama, to the left the European shore splits like a harelip.

A long time ago it was thought that the harelip needed a name and someone likened it to the horn of an ox, or a horn of abundance, a Cornucopia, overflowing with the fruits of the world, also spreading the appealing falsehood that Alexander the Great quenched his thirst here, and adding the qualifier 'golden', which while perhaps not preposterous then, certainly is now, the Golden Horn being full of foundry slag.

A busy water where sea, strait and horn meet. Hundreds of skiffs loaded with sacks, vats, barrels, skins and jars. Huge transports with pitched roofs and fluttering pennants and small windows so the slaves can breathe. Here is the chamberlain of the ambassador of Genoa, standing erect at the prow of his master's barge and holding a tall staff away from his body, pretending to be Andrea Doria pretending to be Neptune.

At this time of year the Sultan's garden is full of Indian violets, purplish in colour with big leaves, a long stem and a sweet smell. From the jetty the royal brig pushes off, fifteen banks of oarsmen in crimson satin over shirts of astonishing whiteness, squaring and feathering, squaring and feathering, as precise as a Hapsburg clock.

On the opposite side of the Horn is the city of Pera, also encircled by a wall, with its warehouses, Genoese tower and magazines of powder and munitions. A crowd at the pier is being entertained by a wild man with a muzzle like a dog whose whole body is covered in thick hair, except the palms of his hands and his knees, and whose owners pull him by an iron chain and oblige him to execute marvellous leaps.

Some fifty Germans and many Italians are at work at the foundry where it is possible to inspect mortars that saw service at Rhodes along with another piece, engraved with figures in relief, that Ibrahim the Frank brought back from the first invasion of Hungary. In the adjacent shipyard they are making two galleys and have wood for several more, destined for the next India campaign.

On the slopes grow vines. Where Alvise Gritti used to live and other Christian plutocrats still do. The monasteries belong to the four mendicant orders and in the chapels one treads on dead Dorias and other Genoese of distinction. In the Monastery of the Visitation the Jesuits do good business in spite of the constant accusations and calumnies of the ambassadors of England, Holland and Venice, but not in the church of St Dominic which the Turks have turned into a mosque. And higher still, amid the juniper, mulberry and acacia trees, the lodge of Yahya the dervish who is the Sultan's elder brother.

One night a bride on a horse is accompanied to her husband's home, preceded by five or six men, with servants on foot, followed by two men carrying wooden candelabra, musicians on horseback, two playing flutes and two the drums, then more men carrying torches. The lady of the occasion wears a veil of red silk and is sheltered under a silken coverlet held up by four corner poles, each pole gripped by a man, a little reminiscent of the Sacrament of King Francis, and with her come five or six attendants bearing her gilded train and some women on horseback, all delivering her to the groom's house and the bridal bed, to be deflowered.

XI

Back in 1453, when Sultan Mehmet took Constantinople from the Byzantines, a typical Ottoman mosque consisted of a roofed box with a minaret up against one of its walls. The Conqueror adopted the Italian dictum that the temples of a great city must be centralised in plan, isolated in a public square and raised on a platform. And he resolved to build 'the best supplied and strongest city ... in power, wealth and glory.' So wrote a witness to his efforts. But try building a new wonder where an old one exists.

Everywhere you look in the city you are reminded that the Byzantines were builders when the Turks were marinating mutton under their saddles and drinking mare's milk for fun. Even those churches that the Ottoman authorities have consciously downgraded and debased, like Christ Chalkites, now a home for painters, St Irene, an armoury, and St John, now the Lion House where the Sultan keeps his wild animals, somehow retain the dignity of their origins.

It's no surprise, therefore, that the mosques that the Turks have built since '53 lack gravitas. The Conqueror's conforms to the footprint of the church it replaced and is let down, quite literally, by its pancake dome. That of his son Bayezid has minarets so far removed from the main structure they might as well belong to another building.

In the former Hippodrome there is a bronze column whose

three serpent heads used to support a gold tripod dedicated to Apollo. Pagan artefacts obviously have no place in a Muslim city but the day after the Conqueror gave one of the three a speculative whack with his scimitar, the Hippodrome was overrun by real snakes, and to prevent a recurrence he ordered that the column be preserved. By the way, if you're wondering why the flocks of ibis that congregate on the columns of the old running track, covering them in shit, may not be killed or molested on pain of death, this too is because they keep snake numbers down.

The biggest obstacle to any sultan who wishes to stamp his Muslim identity on the city is the colossus he cannot dismantle, any more than he can dry up the Bosporus. 'The great door of the newly-built temple groaned on its opening hinges,' an observer wrote of Aya Sofya on 26 December 537, when the Emperor Justinian brought his people to the basilica for the first time, 'and when the first glow of light ... leapt from arch to arch, driving away the dark shadows ... it seemed as if the mighty arches were set in heaven.'

~

Coming ashore after his eventful voyage from Provence, the almoner Jerome Maurand enters the basilica through doors of Corinth bronze and is accosted by a cleric in a turban, dressed in black and wielding a fan of palm leaves, who would like to know on whose authority a priest has crossed the threshold of this Muslim place of worship.

The cleric accepts a gift of thirty aspers and while discussions continue the sun pours in from the lantern windows onto marble meadows that wave and dance, green stone from Haemos, blood-striped from the Iasian Peaks, yellow from Lydia, crocus-gold from Libya and Tyrian purple. And the dome and semidomes, the vaults of the narthex, aisles and gallery, more than four acres in total, shine with gold mosaic.

'All around are chapels,' Maurand observes, 'with very beautiful marble vaults, as big as the body of the church ...

superimposed with divers foliage and birds very beautiful to see. We were unable to see inside, because, as the cleric said, they are always closed, all save one which he showed us, named after St Job, where every Friday the [Sultan] comes to say his prayers, and he told us that in his chapel there are numerous relics of Christian saints, above all the body of Job, and wood from the true Cross in a silver crucifix. Spread on the pavement are rush mats, for the Turks who come in to pray must leave off their shoes or sandals . . .'

This building with a personality disorder. It's unsettling to think of the Sultan's forehead touching the floor of a chapel that contains a fragment of the True Cross. And the Muslim's suspicions of the Christian visitor are surely justified. Priests don't come all the way from France to concede defeat but give secret prayer for Constantinople's liberation when the church that hibernates under Islamic winter will receive the inevitable spring.

Even now, a full ninety years after the Conquest, the Sultan's Muslim subjects haven't got used to the city's Muslim name, Istanbul, which calls to mind the Turkish phrase *Islambol*, meaning 'full of Islam', but continue to call it Konstantiniyye following the example of their Greek neighbours. When architects in Italy draw maps and sketches of Aya Sofya they leave out the minarets, as if this isn't the supreme imperial mosque of the Ottoman Empire, as if the city isn't full of Islam, as if the Conquest never happened.

It's time for the Turks to bin Byzantium and build a proper Islamic metropolis. The muscle and money are there. But where is the architect? Well, there's a question. Istanbul cannot simply lure proven talent from flourishing city states as Rome did when it brought Michelangelo from Florence to work on the new St Peter's. The empire doesn't work that way. That said, there is a precedent from ancient Roman times when distinguished military engineers went on to receive civic and religious commissions. Vitruvius, for example, who left behind a useful book of architectural rules, a copy of which may be consulted in the Sultan's library. And as Vitruvius learned when he was one of Julius Caesar's artillerymen, nothing spurs creativity quite like building fortifications, bridges, catapults and warships under a hail of arrows.

~

The Janissaries have come a long way from their origins as a group of Christian captives being dragged around Anatolia waiting to be ransomed. These men without parents and without children are married to the company whose insignia is tattooed upon their bodies. Murderous efficiency on the battlefield and no home to go back to make for volatile peacetimes. The Janissaries keep order when they are not rioting, they fight fires when they are not setting them, they swear loyalty to the Sultan when they are not overthrowing him and sending him to his death.

They wear billowy trousers in the Hungarian style tied with a ribbon below the knee. They have a strap over the instep of their shoes and a small iron buckle to one side, the better to tighten or widen them. If they see a non-Janissary who is shod in this manner they relieve him of his strap and buckle, beat him and take his money. From their white felt caps they hang a small spoon signifying the brotherhood of men who eat together.

Each company carries the name of its palace duty regardless of what it does on the battlefield. The sixty-fourth is responsible for the hunting dogs, the sixty-ninth for the greyhounds and falcons, while the seventy-first looks after the bearhounds. Superstition is not unknown among the corps. A Janissary never leaves a spoon on the table. A Janissary never steps on a threshold.

Even on campaign they receive fresh bread daily in addition to the basic ration of meat, rice and butter. The sheep and goats that are driven alongside their marching columns are in their prime and the three-year-old mutton is to die for. The company cook is also responsible for discipline in the ranks and, because he is an experienced butcher, doubles up as company executioner.

Perhaps it has something to do with their being converts, or seeing the world from ground level, but the Janissaries do not oppose technological innovation and willingly learn from their enemies. They took to the musket while fighting the Kosovars, who were advanced for the 1380s, and made it their own. By contrast cavalry forces tend to dislike novelty, such as the Egyptian Mamluk horsemen who are attached to their bows and arrows and say sniffily, 'guns can kill fifty men without fighting.' The Janissaries' arquebus volleys did for the Mamluks at Aleppo in 1516, just as they did for the Hungarian heavy cavalry at Mohacs a decade later.

When Mehmet the Conqueror marched on Trabzon, then in Greek hands, in 1461, the rain turned the tracks to a morass. Seeing that his men were unable to advance through the waist-high mud, the Conqueror made a bonfire of his wagons and had the supplies loaded onto eight hundred camels. A Treasury camel fell off a cliff and sixty thousand gold pieces were dispersed over the mountainsides, trousered by the Janissaries. They jangled all the way to Trabzon which they took after a six-week siege. A well-rewarded Janissary is the best infantryman in the world.

~

Not every Janissary has what it takes to be a specialist. If you fail to grasp what is being said when your fellow novice reads aloud from a book explaining the rare and agreeable science of geometry, you will be incapable of attaining expertise and skill as an architect, let alone master the related art of mother-of-pearl inlay. In order to gain acceptance you may be asked to hit a marked spot with an adze upon which your comrades congratulate you with the words, 'May your hand and arm be strong! God, whose name be exalted, bless you with long life! It is your right to be a master of the arts of architecture and the working of mother-of-pearl.'

One who hit the mark in the second decade of the current century was Sinan. A native of Karaman, the central Anatolian province of which Prince Selim is now Governor, he isn't to be confused with Barbarossa's captain Sinan the Jew, but was born under the cross in a village where Armenians and Greeks live in caves cut from the rock. In his teenage years he was included in the boy levy and taken to Istanbul where he was lodged in a dormitory for Janissary cadets near the barracks known as the Old Chambers. There, as he recalls, he 'became desirous [to join] the quarter of carpentry, given the straight-edge of my straight-lined natural disposition.' Apprenticed to a carpenter called Yusuf, 'I remained fixed like a compass, keeping an eye on centre and orbit. Then, as the compass draws an arc, so I desired to tour countries.'

Join the Janissaries, see the world. There's hardly a campaign of note that Sinan wasn't involved in, starting with Sultan Selim's invasion of Iran in 1514. There's hardly a civilisation whose downspouts and coping stones he hasn't seen up close.

The bridge over the Prut in 1538 was his breakthrough. The one that the Sultan's regular engineers built 'sank in the mud and water and disappeared without a trace,' he writes. Within ten days of receiving the royal order, 'I had built a noble bridge [and] the army of Islam and the monarch crossed it with felicity.' His double-walled, double-gated fortress on the Dniester was similarly admired.

In 1539 a tomb was needed for Ayas Pasha of the forty cots. Sinan's name came up and the notables asked, 'would he accept? Is it right that he abandon his career?' The commander of the Janissaries summoned Sinan and told him that he had been appointed to be the Sultan's architect. 'Are you agreeable? If not, find an excuse!'

In Sinan's words, 'the thought of abandoning my career [as a Janissary] gave me great pain but in the end I accepted, seeing in it an opportunity to build many mosques and thereby fulfil many desires in this world and the next.'

And so this ex-troglodyte whose only fault is his *faiblesse* for puns becomes the Sultan's Michelangelo. And while building Hurrem's complex at the Women's Market he receives the most poignant of all commissions, the tomb of a prince.

~

According to the official record of Manisa, at the beginning of the month of Shaban 950, which is to say nine hundred and fifty years after the Prophet migrated from Mecca to Medina, or, to use the calendar of the unbelievers, the penultimate day of October 1543, a state messenger brings news that the Hungarian fortress of Esztergom has fallen to the armies of Islam and Prince Mehmet orders a firework display to celebrate his father's latest acquisition.

It's a matter of days since the Prince bade farewell to Hurrem, Mihrimah and Cihangir who have been staying with him here in Manisa. This place where Hafsa oversaw young Suleyman's court-in-miniature and where she stopped him when he wanted to try on the poisoned robe. Where Mahidevran, not Hurrem, was in his eye and where Mustafa, not Mehmet, took his first breath. A place of mixed feelings, then, for the Sultan's wife. And what is Mahidevran doing right now in Amasya if not protecting her son from being poisoned and keeping him away from plague-afflicted people? Which begs the question, the pestilence having arrived with full force in Manisa, could Hurrem not have delayed her departure from the city and stayed by Mehmet's side? Why did she neglect the duty of every mother, which is to shield her young?

On the same day that he learns of the fall of Esztergom, while the squibs pop, Prince Mehmet notices the swelling in his armpit. His mother is halfway to the capital. His father is returning obliviously from Hungary. The illness takes its course and his death is a lonely one after seven days of unspeakable torment, unattended by any member of his family and knowing he will never see his unborn child.

~

The route from Manisa to Istanbul is supposed to be taken by a man who is coming in all vigour to assume the sabre of the Ottomans, not the body of a sweet boy who died before his time.

Courtiers in black await at Uskudar on the Asian side of the Bosporus. Accompanied by dervishes who chant litanies affirming the oneness of God and the unity of his creation, they receive the body and bring it across the strait to Istanbul. The funeral rites are performed in the mosque of Bayezit and alms are distributed to the poor. Then the body is taken to its designated place of burial, a pleasant place and purified abode in the middle of the city where the Old Chambers used to stand.

No one has seen the Sultan like this. Not when Hafsa died, nor any of his other offspring who died in childhood. His chief secretary likens his madness to that of the Prophet Jacob upon learning of the death of Joseph. With the difference that on this occasion the news is true. The Sultan weeps without interruption for two and a half hours and for a long time he won't let anyone bury his Mehmet, who stood in his library, who gave him news, who chided him for listening to others.

As the poet in him puts it,

> If you rejoice for an instant you will mourn for years,
> Rescue me from the hand of the relentless world.

Yes, the Sultan's verses have a renunciant flavour. And no one can doubt that the Ottoman Empire is a creation of the divine will. The successes it has enjoyed are proof of that. It's the problems that are human.

~

A memorial mosque aids the salvation of the soul, is a consolation to the bereft and evokes the heavenly abode of the deceased. A centralised domical space is appropriate to this limitless state of being. A Latin Cross, with its running limbs and hierarchy of closeness to the false idol, is not.

'There is no art more difficult than architecture and whosoever is engaged in this estimable calling . . . should not begin to lay the foundations if the building site is not firm, and . . . he should take great care that his work be free from defect and he reach the firm ground.' So writes Sinan. 'In proportion to the abundance or paucity of piers, columns and buttresses, he should close up the domes and half domes that are on top of them, and bind the arches together in an agreeable manner, without carelessness. And he should not hurry in important matters but should endure in accord with . . . the saying, "Patience brings one victory!"'

Try urging patience on a pair of high-maintenance clients who are fretting for the soul of their son, the father insisting that there isn't a moment to waste, the mother with her unscheduled site visits. But Sinan is a Janissary and if his thoughts ever turn to his predecessor Atik Sinan, whose pancake dome for the Conqueror was rewarded with his arrest and murder in custody, he doesn't let it show.

There is no confusion on site but a purposeful hum that reminds one of Barbarossa's men coming ashore at Toulon, with the difference that this commander-in-chief carries a cubit measure, not a sword. Doing his rounds Sinan issues orders to masters of the glaziers, lead-sheet makers, marble cutters, bricklayers, lime-burners, blacksmiths, whitewashers and layers of water channels. The labourers are driven on by Janissary captains who lay siege to the site and tuck their skirts into their belts and will not rest until Azadlu stone, Gallipoli brick, Black Sea timber, Macedonian lead, Samokov iron and recycled English brass have given up their individual properties and submitted to the scheme. There has been a glut of English brass ever since King Henry started stripping his monasteries and churches of their Popish accessories.

Yes, it takes more than money to transform the former site of a barracks into an earthly paradise featuring not only a Friday mosque but also a mausoleum for the Prince's remains, a school of religious sciences, a hospice, a guest house and a Quran school for children, and all this in landscaped gardens planted with cypresses and oriental planes. A lot of cleverness, a lot of government, a lot of God.

~

When it is finished, the intimate mausoleum preserves the boy's vivacity in the flutes of its dome and the exterior walls that are alive with red sandstone and coloured marble. The interior makes one want to smile or even dance for the sarcophagus is afloat in an ocean of light strained through sixteen windows full of coloured glass and the interior walls are covered in tiles whose dominant colour is the apple green of youth. Whenever the chief mourner visits in his caftan of black watered silk he emerges refreshed with the moon-like face of the smiling boy in his mind's eye.

The mosque itself is a feat of geometry, the architect's sure hand showing in the harmony of the two squares of which it is composed, the one a perfectly proportioned dome raised on four polygonal piers, the other an arcaded courtyard. Note the assuredness with which the architect arranges his lesser domes and half domes around the central dome, like the foothills of a lofty mountain. And in contrast with the mosque of Bayezid, whose minarets distract the eye from the cube at its heart, those of the Mosque of the Prince stand in close attendance, needles knitting together the squares.

Of the mosque's many praiseworthy features it is these minarets that evoke the sunbursts of youth. They boast not one but two honeycombed galleries in recognition of the late prince's status as heir apparent, and in their decorative exuberance they are without precedent in this or any other Ottoman city, being carved with a profusion of crescents, stars, knots and rosettes. At night they are lit using oil lamps set into the galleries so that people notice them from far away and pray for the soul of the Pick of Princes, the name his father remembers him by.

~

Is it any surprise that this year, 1543, the year he grieves, returns from his tenth campaign and enters his sixth decade, is the year he tires of war?

To paraphrase Rustem Pasha, the wars of the Christians are bagatelles, conducted close to home and with all ease, while the Sultan must cover half the earth before he even finds an enemy, and when he eventually returns to Istanbul he leaves behind a third of his army, men and horses, sick or dead.

No longer is there talk of wintering in Buda and 'next year, Vienna'. In the words of no less an observer than Gerard Velt-wyck, the Emperor's envoy, 'the [Sultan] thinks more of living into old age than he does of further conquest; and the Sultana exhorts him to stay at home.' Sultana is the name by which the Europeans know the Sultan's wife. That and Roxelana, from her background in the 'little Russia' of Ruthenia.

In the spring of 1544 the Sultan orders a party to Geyikli Baba on the mountain near Bursa, to hunt and enjoy the baths there. The most significant inclusion in the party is Prince Selim, who recently became a father to a daughter, Ismihan Sultan, and is summoned from Karaman. Hurrem, Mihrimah, Bayezid, Rustem Pasha and Hadim Suleyman, who is hanging on as Grand Vizier, are the other members of the party. The most significant omission is Prince Mustafa.

Often the most important decisions are taken on holiday. As the chronicler puts it, 'the Sultan of the world, the Alexander of the age, took Prince Selim with him to drink from the running water of life and to contemplate the world from the world-seeing summit and the Prince shone and glowed in reflection of the dawn on the lofty mountain. They exerted themselves to reach the heaven-resembling peak and having ascended to and descended from the summit which brings spiritual refreshment . . .

hunted . . . and the sun of the world turned favourably towards the moon at his side.'

After forty days the sun of the world returns to the capital. And the moon travels west to assume his functions as Governor of Manisa and the mantle of heir apparent.

~

Charles's adviser Nicolas Perrenot de Granvelle tells his master, 'there is, sire, a maxim in affairs of state, just as in other matters: that one must pay attention to the reality of the matters under discussion, to determine what is possible and what God and reason suggest is attainable, rather than take big risks because of personal considerations.'

In truth the Emperor long ago let his policy towards the Turks lag behind his sentiments. 'When the Sultan advanced against Vienna,' he told a Venetian diplomat back in '38, 'we saw that it is not always possible to force him to battle when one wishes, yet he commands so many horsemen that he can advance and retire, and devastate the countryside, at will.' Since then he has favoured a defensive posture in those parts of northern and western Hungary that remain in Hapsburg hands and constitute Vienna's curtain wall, improving strongholds and installing garrisons but otherwise not committing troops for campaigns.

Strongholds that turn out to be far from invulnerable. Each time the Sultan marches against Ferdinand, redoubts fall and more people are persuaded that orderly Turkish government is preferable to the inefficient despotism that the pro-Hapsburg magnates are offering. So writes Gerard Veltwyck, also noting that the Hungarian peasants 'have not been so oppressed by the Turks as they are daily by the Hungarian lords, and . . . praise marvellously their treatment' at Turkish hands. These same peasants even 'betray their [Hungarian] lords to the Turks and have them killed or taken prisoner'.

Not only are the Hapsburgs losing Hungary, they are losing their German heartland to the Lutherans. No imperial diet, no appeal to unity, has sufficed to smother the sedition, and certainly not the poorly attended Church council that finally convenes in 1545 at Trent in the Tyrol. It is a measure of how contagious Lutheran ideas are that one of the early champions of a church council, Pietro Paolo Vergerio, who in 1535 endured that indigestible breakfast with Luther, was recently interrogated by the Venetian Inquisition on suspicion of having gone over to the heresy!

For the past twenty-five years the Hapsburg brothers have pointed their pikes south and their mouths north. It is time to invert this arrangement; if not, all of Hungary will be lost and there won't be such a thing as a Catholic German.

And the Sultan has long been looking for an excuse to give up his frontier fortresses which are so costly to supply. In the words of the ever bribable, ever consummate Yunus Bey, 'since the time of Ibrahim Pasha [the Sultan] has been unhappy with his conquest of Hungary and has always said that as soon as he is able to come out of this war with honour, that is to say, when [Ferdinand's ambassadors] come to him with tribute, he will accept.'

What did Suleyman advise the Most Christian King? That 'only by fighting with resolve will the enemy be forced to sue for peace.' And who would argue that he hasn't followed his own advice, swallowing most of Hungary, terrorising the coasts of the White Sea and sitting comfortably while the Emperor founders at Algiers?

Suleyman will not send diplomats to European courts. He will not put up in the Louvre. On the contrary, the resolve he has demonstrated over the past quarter of a century has reduced his rival to the status of a supplicant. And when Gerard Veltwyck receives his document of safe passage to Constantinople, the Dutchman writes, 'never was a lord of the Turks so happy as this one, seeing that so great a prince . . . sends an embassy to their country.'

~

Negotiations get going in late 1544 and the Hapsburgs immediately grasp that while the Sultan is indifferent to all gifts except clocks, the ladies of the court are not. The Emperor advises Veltwyck to reserve his best charm for the Sultana, who is known to rule the Sultan and may be approached through her eunuchs and Jewish attendants, and to 'give her to understand that we will look kindly on all that concerns her, and her children'.

Charles and Ferdinand have asked the French to mediate in the negotiations. Which suits Francis up to a point because the Sultan was offended by the anti-Turkish clauses in the Treaty of Crepy which the Most Christian King wishes to make up for. 'Up to a point,' because he dreads a Hapsburg–Ottoman accord that diminishes his influence in Turkish affairs. So the diplomats he sends to Istanbul work as diligently to delay an agreement as they do to promote it.

Far away in Wittenberg Luther denounces the peace talks as a betrayal of Christendom. Brother Martin is sixty and his ailments, which include a sore leg, gout, constipation, urine retention and a continuous headache, are not exclusively alcohol-related. The Emperor, he writes, the King of France, the Pope and Ferdinand 'have sent embassies loaded with costly gifts for the Turk. And there they are, on the road to Istanbul, these Roman swindlers, and this is how they make war against the Turk, whom they have for so many years called the enemy of the Christian name, against whom the Roman Satan has drained off such a vast sum of money in indulgences, annates and infinite rapacities. Now you see the ruin of the Empire at hand and the day of our salvation. Let us be glad, rejoice, exult – the end of the world is coming!'

In fact Pope Paul has sent no envoy. But he is keeping a close eye on what happens in Istanbul having promised the Emperor money and men for the coming campaign against the Lutherans. Yes, peace on the Bosporus will birth war on the Rhine. And maybe other offspring. The Portuguese are pressing for a side-treaty on Indian trade. The Venetians want to ringfence their trading rights and the French are begging a loan of thirty thousand ducats.

In the course of the negotiations the serial bullshitter Christoph von Roggendorf, son of the twice-foiled besieger of Buda, defects to the Sultan with eight thousand ducats stolen from his ex-wife and promising half of Austria which isn't in his gift. Christoph's refusal to convert reminds the Sultan of the last infidel who promised the earth and ended up betraying him. One Alvise Gritti is enough. Sensing danger the Austrian escapes under cover of darkness but is intercepted before he can reach the safety of Venetian Cyprus and is brought back to Istanbul in chains. The French ambassador, knowing his master to be a less severe judge of character than the Sultan, arranges Christoph's release from the Seven Towers and his passage to France where he embarks on the next phase of his career of chicanery, this time in the service of the Most Christian King.

~

Whenever the diplomats are not outbribing each other in their meetings with the Pashas or presenting gems woven with gold to be passed to Mihrimah, they get lost in the Covered Market where in addition to Salina raisins and Chios mastic they are liable to be offered Christian slaves including children as young as eight who are led about by the hand and sold to the highest bidder. Whenever a buyer appears for a particular female she is taken to a corner and her veil is lifted so that the buyer may examine her teeth and enquire about her age, place of origin and virginity, as happened to Roxelana who now lives up the road in improved circumstances. And the diplomats pride themselves on buying such slaves in order to set them at liberty, perhaps forgetting that they themselves were rowed across the Adriatic by fettered Muslims.

Another attraction is the Lion House where it is possible to see one of God's more singular creatures, called by some people a sea pig and by others a sea cow, though neither name does justice to this car crash of an animal which hails from the Nile, has a head like an ox but without horns, small ears, a long fat body, stumpy legs, a tough hairless hide and a face like sin. Also among the animals in the Lion House is an ancient elephant whose pastimes include fencing with its Moorish keeper and eating a velvet cap sewn with gold buttons that it snatched from the head of the treasurer of the French galleys, the gentleman in question being advised by the laughing Moor that he will be able to retrieve every last button if he waits for nature to take its course.

This city of dung and water which is so much bigger than Paris, Vienna or Madrid. This theatre in the round where one hundred and fifty of the Captain Pasha's slaves abscond in a boat having stolen fifteen thousand of his hard-earned ecus and are pursued by six galleys; where one must resign oneself to a perpetual hammering and an inexpungeable film of dust because the chief architect won't stop building mosques, schools, public fountains and water-channels; and where, on 19 June 1547, Suleyman's calligraphic emblem is fixed to a treaty that sells the Christians peace and the Hapsburgs a string of high-maintenance border fortresses in return for an annual tribute of thirty thousand ducats. The Venetians are folded into the treaty, as is the Pope and the French who are rewarded not with cash but Cairene saltpetre. Only the Portuguese go away empty-handed. The Sultan doesn't pay protection.

~

Like Turkish viziers, French princes are promoted one funeral at a time. When Francis's eldest son, also called Francis, died in 1536, the boy's younger brother Henry, Duke of Orleans, replaced him as Dauphin and the third brother, Charles, Duke of Angouleme, was promoted to Duke of Orleans.

In the autumn of 1545, while he waits to find out which Hapsburg he will marry, the Duke of Orleans is in northern France to repel a pointless English invasion in the course of which he commandeers a house that is thought to be infected. 'Never a son of France was killed by the plague,' he laughs, slashing a quilt with his sword and covering himself with feathers. Soon afterwards he falls ill and when his condition worsens his father cannot be restrained from coming to his side. 'My lord,' the stricken prince whispers when Francis enters the chamber, 'I die, but since I see your Majesty I die content.' In the words of the Emperor's ambassador, who witnesses the scene, Francis 'wept for a long time, crying loudly and shedding tears in great quantity' and moaning that God is punishing him for his sins.

On 9 September, while the Emperor is travelling to Brussels to invest Charles of Orleans with the Duchy of Milan, he learns of the boy's death and muses that it will allow him to keep both Milan and the Netherlands and that this news 'came at such a good time that it might seem as if God had arranged it for his secret purposes'. But the Emperor is also a father and the letter of condolence he sends Francis so touches the King that he replies in his own hand praying that 'God will be gracious to you so that you may never need such comfort nor feel what pain it is to lose a son.'

Act Four: The Cabal

XII

The Sultan's Lutherans are called the red-headed ones for the
roll of scarlet cloth, more than half an ell long, which they coil
around their heads. They revere the Prophet's cousin and son-
in-law Ali above the Prophet himself and for this reason they
are also known as the partisans of Ali, or Shias. In the morning
when the Supreme Guide of their Safavid order goes to his place
of audience, he is preceded by a man who rains loud curses on
the Companions of the Prophet, much loved by all Sunnis
including the members of the House of Osman. In the evening
it is said that they 'snuff out the candle', which is to say that
their alcohol-fuelled ceremonies wrap up with an orgy.

The Safavid name comes from the order's founder, Safi al-
Din, whose descendent Tahmasp, the current Supreme Guide, is
Shah of Iran. Tahmasp's followers in Ottoman Anatolia live as
if they are his subjects and not the Sultan's. Forget supplying
men for Suleyman's campaigns, they rebel against him inces-
santly and send his rival a tax called the 'Shah's due', and
Tahmasp in turn sends missionaries among them, bringing a
warrant, a cloak, a sword and silver tumans minted in his capital, Tabriz. When the red-headed ones go on pilgrimage it isn't
to Mecca but to Safi al-Din's mausoleum in Iran.

Sultan Selim was among the first to recognise the gravity of
the threat posed by the red-headed ones to the Ottoman state.
Armed with a fatwa authorising their pursuit using falcons,

arrows and dogs, he slaughtered forty thousand of them in Anatolia alone. In 1514 he entered Iran and defeated Tahmasp's father, Shah Ismail, in battle. But the Persian plateau, while easy to penetrate, is hard to hold on to, and Selim was soon forced home again.

When he was a ten-year-old Ismail's son Tahmasp would drink as hard as his father and after inheriting the kingdom he made a show of killing with his own hands lions, bears and men. Recently he received a visit by saintly apparitions as a result of which he outlawed alcohol, hashish and sodomy; his latest hobby is fishing for brown trout. The Shah's three brothers are Bahram Mirza, who drinks a good deal, has many handsome page boys and ignores the new prohibitions, Sam Mirza, who has no power but a title, Emperor of Constantinople, and no beard, and Alqas Mirza who is the Shah's favourite brother and governs the province of Shirvan on the western shore of the Caspian Sea. Tahmasp's sister Mahinbanu Sultan is unmarried having been reserved for the Mahdi or guided one, whose reappearance after five centuries of occultation is expected any time now.

In 1535 Sultan Suleyman marched against Tahmasp and took Baghdad from him but the Shah avoided meeting him in battle, thereby living to fight another day. Since then the Sultan has been busy in Hungary allowing the Shah to pursue his policies of terrorising Sunnis at home and winning converts abroad, while also spurring an exodus of Anatolian Shias into territory under his control.

In 1540 a Venetian diplomat called Michele Membre witnessed the arrival of four thousand such migrants at Tabriz. In Membre's words, the tribesmen rode 'round and round; all together they kept crying, 'Allah, Allah,' until the Shah came forth from his apartments ... then he ordered the greatest of their chiefs to be summoned, and, one by one, they came and kissed the foot of the said Shah ... then the said [tribesmen] gave presents to the Shah, each, according to his means, so many animals: some gave horses, some wethers and some camels. Then the Shah ordered them to three parts of his lands, that is, he sent one part to the province of Khurasan, another part to the province of Shirvan, and the other part to the province of Iraq.' In other words, to the eastern, northern and western extremities of his domains.

Suleyman is aware of the seductive powers of the heresy, writing in a poem, 'I am frightened that blasphemy's tresses will entice me away from religion; oh God, do not mix blasphemers among the people of Islam . . . do not let the Muslims become captive to the heretics.' For the Sultan an eastern offensive doesn't have the frisson of a dust-up with the Christians but is a fraught and sombre duty against the enemy within. Long marches through barren and wasted lands, the difficulty of telling friend from foe and the Iranians' tactic of mounting lightning ambushes on swift horses are the features. Nor can Iran, huge and uncontainable, be easily invaded and the problem solved that way. As Suleyman himself wrote of his campaign against Tahmasp back in '35, 'I embarked on the journey out of zeal for Islam, God knows that I did not undertake these campaigns to acquire worldly possessions.'

Suleyman's new Mufti, who oversees the doctors of the law, is Ebussuud Efendi. For eight years Ebussuud was the chief judge of the army of Rumelia. He is also the author of a great commentary on the Quran and his palace at Sutluce on the Horn is advantageously placed opposite the tomb of Eyup, the Prophet's comrade-in-arms. In one of his fatwas, Ebussuud describes a convent in which boys undermine the unity of God with numerous melodies, crying out, 'my soul, my heart' and uttering such invocations as, 'You can give paradise to those who desire a houri, what I need is only you!' while beating their breasts and making strange gestures. Ebussuud has ruled that a sheikh who permits such rituals is a heretic and that if he and his disciples refuse to give up these practices they must be executed.

The Efendi has also ruled that every Muslim village must have a prayer hall and every town a mosque so that people may perform the congregational prayers according to the Hanafi school that is the basis of Ottoman law. And yet across Anatolia many of the new religious buildings are empty because the people reject the legitimacy of the religious authorities who administer them. On the other side of the Iranian border the red-headed ones remember with affection a chuntering pig that Shah Ismail kept at court, called Bayezit after the present Sultan's grandfather. Yes, the Iranians trade in insult as well as injury and Suleyman's new peace with the Hapsburgs has given him a breathing space in which to come up with a reply. So when in the summer of 1547 Tahmasp's brother Alqas Mirza defects, offering him a Sunni Iran, the Sultan is receptive.

Tahmasp raised Alqas above his other brothers and named him Shirvanshah, or king of Shirvan. But members of Alqas's entourage incited him to rebel and he minted coins and had sermons read in his name. Tahmasp marched north with his emirs and when they caught up with Alqas he galloped off and, embarking at the Sea of Azov, made for Istanbul.

The Sultan is spending more and more time at Edirne, ten days' journey into Thrace, where the winters are softer and the deer come up to the window. Informed that the Sultan is out of town, the Prince addresses a letter to 'his highness the viceregent of the heavenly step of lofty Saturn', 'the founder of the pedestal of the Caesars' and 'the exalter of the tablets of justice and beneficence'. He also calls Suleyman the 'occupant of the throne of King Solomon' and the 'bestower of crowns on the heads of kings'. And when he is done placing watermelons under the Sultan's arms, as the Persian saying goes, he gets to the point.

'My brother, the occupant of the dynastic throne of this sincere friend, arranged for a number of mischief-makers to engage in corruption and deception and they laid a trap of duplicity and knavery in the path of this humble slave.' While Alqas was away campaigning, he goes on, Tahmasp marched on Shirvan and 'attacked the men, women and children of Islam and stripped all the offspring of Islam of their possessions, and when news of what had happened reached this sincere friend I ... came to this land.'

The Prince closes with an appreciation of Suleyman's green

fingers. 'I am as dust and thorns and you are the sun and the clouds. I will give roses and tulips if you tend to me.'

The Sultan recently received the ambassador of Alaeddin, an Indian ruler, who gave him parrots, spices, balms and a cannibal eunuch. Alqas offers only promises. But what promises! After the invasion, he tells the Sultan, the coins of Iran will be 'struck and adorned with the supreme name' of Suleyman and 'the pulpits of Islam in the land of Iran will resound to the most noble titles of that royal highness'. And to demonstrate his sincerity he renounces the Shia faith and embraces Sunnism, also assuring the Sultan that 'in their hearts the tribes of the red-headed ones support me. I have only to set foot on Persian soil and they will flock to me.'

~

When Suleyman returns to Istanbul from Edirne, accompanied by his army, he makes sure that Alqas is seated on a tribune by the side of the road. First the armourers file past and when their commander reaches Alqas's tribune the Prince assumes that this splendid figure is the Sultan and he rises to his feet before realising his error and sitting down again. One after another the commanders of the artillery, cavalry, light infantry and Janissaries go past with their men and Alqas repeats his mistake again and again, each time looking more of a fool. By the time Suleyman finally appears amid a forest of golden lances and bonnets, helmets and panaches, the Prince is a wreck.

Having awed his guest it is time to fatten him up. The chimneys of the New Palace pump out woodsmoke with results that include a dish made of the flesh of birds, with cumin seeds and vinegar, grilled mutton, lamb, quail, duck, chicken and goose, rice dishes featuring pulses, fruit and nuts, stuffed aubergines, pastries made with sour dough, almond oil, kidney beans and yoghurt, fritters, soups made from pomegranate molasses, marzipans, a yellow dessert made with saffron and rice that is familiar to the Prince, being Persian in origin, jellied fruits and much else, but nothing to suit the palate of the cannibal eunuch.

And so smooth and practised is the Ottoman welcome, so finely poised between humility and condescension, that among the chests full of gold and silver and the teams of black and white slaves that Alqas receives from his host, the gold and silver vessels, Arab horses and harnesses embroidered with precious stones, there are shirts, quilts and sheets with brocade tassels that the Sultan's wife has lovingly sewn her royal brother.

'What is the necessity of such . . . expense?' grumble the doctors of the law; 'for this man isn't here to show his respect for Sunnism, but to save his skin. What is more he remains a godless heretic deep down and to bring him among the Muslims is an unadulterated harm.' When this criticism reaches the ears of the Sultan, he shrugs, saying, 'We did what the honour of the state required and if someone has betrayed his religion he will be punished by mighty God.'

~

In early 1548, for the eleventh time, Suleyman's seven horsetails surmounted by gilded pommels are planted at the gate of the New Palace to announce the forthcoming campaign. On 8 April, a date determined by his astrologer, he rides out preceded by Prince Cihangir, the first time his youngest and least robust son has joined him on campaign. The trumpets and kettledrums strike up and from the arsenal there is a terrific cannonade as father and son are conveyed across the Bosporus to Uskudar and the waiting army.

Riding eastwards Suleyman ascends the tableland of Asia Minor, following hills and rivers that are signposted by poplars and willows, a country so well washed it will never want for water, so well cultivated it will never want for food, so full of wishing trees it will never want for God. The villages are like the ninety-nine cornelians on a string of prayer beads, neither too close together nor too far apart, and the turf is rolling, hard-bitten and dun.

The irony is that it's the Sultan's Christians who live loyal, quiet, industrious lives and the Muslim tribes whose enthusiasms

have to be monitored, curbed and chastised, their lodges infil-
trated and repeat offenders sent to Istanbul for trial and
punishment. How many of his subjects, the Sultan perhaps
wonders as he skirts villages that make up his hinterland and
yet are less familiar than those of the well-trodden Danubian
plain, curse him and his family and the pioneers of Islam?

Passing through Phrygia he visits the tomb of Seyyid Battal,
who took part in the second Arab siege of Constantinople, in
718, and was martyred in a later engagement with the Byzantines. Under the dome at Konya he communes with Rumi who
urged the suicide of the self in an ocean of divine love. 'What
men call the sultanate is but a fight over the world,' runs the
Sultan's reply; 'there is no luck and happiness in the world com-
pared to unity with God or closeness to God.'

Every king longs to close his eyes and never open them again.
It comes with the territory. And every king is a prisoner of baser
realms of existence; he sits on a low throne. What could be
lower than Muslims marching against Muslims and a foe whose
betrayal of his own brother makes him a friend? As the Ottoman chroniclers attest, the enmity of siblings is an evil legacy of
Cain and Abel that is being perpetuated by the Safavids. What
they avoid mentioning is that this same abomination is the
Ottoman mother clause, the dead dog releasing its poison
beneath the milk-white surface of the state.

As the Sultan makes his way across Anatolia he has the pleasure of being met by his three able-bodied sons, Selim in Phrygia,
Bayezit and Mustafa further east. The former is sent to Edirne
to mind the shop, the latter pair being deputed to suppress any
rebellion of the red-headed ones that may break out in central
Anatolia while the Sultan is away – and how strange it must be
to stop and reflect that what is happening is a review and audi-
tion of the actors in his own blood-stained succession! It is
already clear that twenty-four year-old Selim, chubby, oversexed and usually hungover, may not be a good fit for the office
that Hurrem's cabal envisages for him. When Suleyman meets
Mustafa after all these years, how can he reconcile the boy's

obvious suitability for the sabre of the Ottomans with the resolve of the cabal to stop him reaching that lofty office? To put it another way, how powerful does one have to be to be truly powerless?

Cihangir is old enough to know what is going on and he ventures to hope that his life will be spared on account of his disability, for, as he says, whoever becomes Sultan 'will have no cause to fear me'. To which his father replies with a brutality that perhaps surprises them both, 'Mustafa will be Sultan and he will kill you all.'

~

And so to war. In the far north-east the knights of Georgia, who have been playing a double game and ally themselves with the Ottomans and the Safavids in turn, come down on their little mounts to kiss a king's passing hand. Turning south, between Erzurum and Lake Van he receives the son of the former ruler of Shirvan who has retaken his homeland and put the red-headed ones to the sword. And after crossing many rivers, including the headwaters of the Euphrates, which flows all the way to the Gulf of Basra, the Sultan enters a land of strongholds and upland pastures that the Turks and Iranians have spent years taking and retaking from each other.

Skirting Van and its Safavid-held fortress, Suleyman is diverted by Alqas eastwards all the way to Tabriz, which on 29 July he enters unopposed as he's done before, in 1535, and his father did in 1514. The Shah has taken the usual precautions, emptying the city of people and food, blocking the underground water-channels and laying waste the surrounding countryside. There is nothing to eat and the death toll of Ottoman beasts of burden quickly reaches five thousand horses, camels and mules.

Back in '35 the Sultan was fired up by fatwas urging him to crush the head of the viper and he continued further into the plateau, finding no enemy but winter which cost him many men on the frozen march south to Baghdad. This time the plan is to instal Alqas as an Ottoman client but when he enters Tabriz the

Prince's supporters set to robbing the city's remaining inhabitants and burn Tahmasp's palace while Alqas himself proposes a general massacre or enslavement.

Hold on. This isn't Lipari where the enemy were Christians and the lines were clear. There are protocols of clemency to observe when the Caliph of Islam apprehends members of his flock who have gone astray. Suleyman sends Rustem to put a stop to the looting but Alqas's rapacity and the lack of food oblige the Ottomans to evacuate the city on the fifth day of the occupation and retrace their steps to Van, which, thanks to the excellence of the Ottoman gunners, who fire balls of marble, iron and steel, and the irresolution of the defenders, who are driven by the ferocity of the assault to lower themselves from the walls using ropes of hemp, soon capitulates.

The autumn of 1548 is a time of revised expectation. No more dreams of a Sunni Iran and the Sultan's head on coins. Just get the Shah and his diabolical gangs of horsemen out of eastern Anatolia which they are turning into a wasteland, burning crops, ambushing Ottoman detachments and slaughtering so much livestock that the people call them 'cow-breakers'. Daily the red-headed ones are augmented by fresh units that arrive from Iran and join with glee in the destruction of the Sultan's possessions.

The answer to asymmetry is guile. Approaching an Iranian force in the vicinity of Erzincan, an Ottoman pasha called Osman orders his men to catch wild sheep from whose tails they hang copper vessels, and crows and ravens which they tie to the tails of their horses. In the dead of night they drive their animal army cawing, bleating, neighing and clanging into the silent camp where the Iranians, awoken by the Day of Judgement, snatch up their weapons and butcher each other in terror and confusion. And the Sultan rewards Osman Pasha with the governorship of Aleppo.

By now he has tired of Alqas whose followers refuse to fight alongside the Turks, and in November he sends the Prince back into Iran with a few thousand malcontents, which has the desired effect for when the Shah hears that his brother is looting the plateau he halts Anatolian operations and heads for home.

Alqas's rabble sweeps through Qom and Kashan but all the riches he sends back to Suleyman from those desert towns, all the Nishapur turquoises, Badakhshan rubies and Khurasan carpets, cannot conceal the fact that his brother's subjects do not support or flock to him. On the contrary, they slam their gates in his face at Isfahan, Shiraz and various towns along the River Karun. And after careering wildly around southern Iran he flees to Ottoman Baghdad where he is not welcome either.

In the autumn of 1549 he is captured by the Iranians and is brought before Tahmasp who says, 'Oh, my unkind brother! What harm have I done you, that you should turn away from your allegiance to your father's house, and should cast yourself down from the zenith of honour to the nadir of baseness, and should make overtures to the enemy, and be responsible for so much sedition, rebellion, and bloodshed?' And Alqas is taken off to a remote prison and thrown from the ramparts.

It is related that while Alqas was in Iraq he wished to go as a pilgrim to Karbala and the shrine of Ali's son the Imam Hussein, who was martyred by Yazid, the Caliph of the time, and is beloved of the Shias. When he arrived at the shrine with its dome of blinding gold, the custodians greeted him with jeers, saying 'you joined the Turks and became Yazid,' and they would not admit him. But he stayed in their company and after a few days he began cursing the Companions of the Prophet as he had done before his conversion to Sunnism, also praying with his hands by his side in the Shia manner. In this way, having betrayed the Islam of the Shah, he betrayed that of the Sultan and no one, perhaps not even himself, knew what kind of Muslim he was any more.

~

From Aleppo the Sultan summons Prince Bayezit from Konya. Falcons, hawks and dogs are brought from distant eyries and kennels. Trained cheetahs, which have the advantage of flexing their backbones and achieving high speeds, arrive on the backs of horses which they cling to skilfully. Other preparations include fencing in a well-watered hillside and notifying villagers lest timid women and others who hold their persons dear take fright. Three hundred gamekeepers and thousands of beaters spend three days and three nights driving hares, foxes, gazelles, wolves, stags, bears, black-faced boars and jackals into the huge enclosure.

Once the hunt is underway the perimeter is contracted by the advancing beaters, who don't exactly honour the notion of the sporting chance, and at times the quarry is so thick that it is hard to see the ground. The larger game is brought down by hounds, including Salukis, a light brown breed of great antiquity with a greyhound's body, hanging ears and a feathered tail and legs. At the water's edge a green-winged duck withdraws its head from its breast and takes to the air but the falcon kills it on the wing and drops it to the ground, where it is retrieved by a mastiff bitch that brings it to the Sultan with a soft mouth as if it were her own pup. In recognition of this the Sultan awards his chief falconer a robe of honour, for did the Mufti not rule that it is forbidden to eat an animal from which a dog has drawn blood?

~

The people become jittery when the Sultan is away for the winter and particularly so when the news from the front is of heavy casualties – as it is also from the home front. On 21 August 1549 Ferdinand's envoy Johann Maria Malvezzi writes to his master, 'every day the pestilence multiplies and in Constantinople alone no fewer than five hundred die daily ... the air itself is thought to be infected for when walking in the street many fall and immediately die.'

On 8 October Malvezzi reports that 'Mustafa the Sultan's eldest son is insisting that [the Sultan] confide the army to him and leave him the burden of the war ... and that [the Sultan] return to Constantinople to rest, but ... Rustem Pasha insists that [the Sultan] do no such thing, suspecting that having taken charge of the army Mustafa will make himself absolute ruler of all.' For lack of money the Sultan 'has melted all his silver plate to make coins, the other Pashas doing the same, and to cover up the fact that such a measure was taken out of necessity the Mufti has ruled that the use of silver plate is forbidden under Islam.'

News reaches Hurrem that the herald will arrive imminently announcing the Sultan's triumphant return and the war's end. But how can this be the case when the Sultan recently sent for more men, horses and artillery? 'My Sultan,' she writes in perplexity, 'the city is in uproar because the herald is [rumoured to be] coming. The whole world stands ready to deck out the city [but] if the herald really were coming, that would be strange, for you, my Sultan, and your government are wintering in Aleppo . . . [the herald] is driving me up the wall before he even gets here!' Then, remembering why her husband has been away for the better part of two years, she begs God to drown the Shah in the deep waters of the Karun.

Two years in the company of Mehmet's daughter Huma Shah and Mihrimah's little girl Aisha. Two years of arguable over-reliance on the family sheikh, Merkez Efendi, the one who invented the paste with occult qualities and who recently discovered a holy well up from the Sea of Marmara. 'Just now a great saint sent news,' she writes, 'that it would have been better if the Sultan had not gone [to war] this year.' On the other hand, the saint goes on, 'by the grace of God from now on victory will be the King's. Let him not be sad for every sadness has its joy.' The words of a sheikh hedging his bets.

Her letters are more to the point than they used to be. They need to be, bearing in mind the impending crisis. 'My felicitous one . . . Rustem Pasha is your slave. Keep him by your side . . . don't listen to what anyone else says.' By which she means, for God's sake don't go soft in the head and hand the army over to Mustafa!

~

Gingerly broaching the question of his longevity, she writes, 'my world and my felicity, my Sultan, how is your auspicious and noble health? Your auspicious head and your whole body and your auspicious foot, are they well? Now, my world, my Sultan, are you in good health? My Sultan, my precious, I beseech the Creator, may he be exalted, to shield your noble body from all mishap and evil, and may you always be under the protection of Allah and live a long life like the Prophet Noah.'

On the way home from Aleppo he is taken ill and his legs hurt him so much that men with sweet voices are ordered to sing outside his tent, not for his pleasure but so that the army will not hear his cries, and Moses Hamon does not know what the cause is, far less the solution. To Mihrimah the Sultan writes, 'my leg hurt for a day or two,' the kind of virile understatement that makes a daughter worry all the more. Ruled out of a side-operation against the Georgians, he is carried to a pasture full of wildflowers near Diyarbakir where a month of being breathed over by perfumed zephyrs restores him to health, if not vigour.

Francis is dead. He died of the French disease. His son Henry has become Most Christian King and his inheritance includes his father's alliance with the Turks. In a letter to the new King, Suleyman announces the success of his eastern campaign. The Muslims of Iran, he writes, 'remain in peace and joy day and night under our obedience ... thank God that the country of the red-headed ones is ruined and uninhabitable.' Well, perhaps. On his way home from the East he lodges with one of his subjects, who, after his departure, considering his house to have been defiled and contaminated, fumigates it and purifies it with lustral water. When Suleyman hears about this, he has the man in question put to death and his house razed, as much in frustration as anger, one suspects, for the campaign has left an unpleasant taste in the mouth along with more dead Sunnis and live Shias than he hoped for.

On 21 December, writes Malvezzi, 'the Turkish Lord entered Constantinople in good health but extremely disgruntled and very old, to the indifferent joy of the people on account of the very unsuccessful conclusion of this Persian war ... in these past two years two thirds of the army have died and the defeat sustained by this Sultan is far greater than I have so far written.'

And it may be argued that the Emperor Charles has made better use of the truce than Suleyman has, routing the Protestants at Muhlberg on the Elbe and capturing Luther's former citadel of Wittenberg where he rejected the Duke of Alba's suggestion that they have some fun with the bones of the monk, who expired two years earlier: 'I don't make war on the dead, only on the living.' Not that the truce has been observed without blemish, by any means, and an ambassador of Queen Isabella informs the Sultan that in Transylvania the King of the Romans has 'taken several castles' and 'sacked and ruined twenty-five or thirty villages' that the Sultan had assigned as fiefs, allegations that Malvezzi unconvincingly denies. The King of the Romans is one of Ferdinand's titles. It signifies that he is his brother's designated heir.

XIII

In the end the Hadim needed dislodging. Rustem arranged a career-ending audit of his financial performance as Governor of Egypt. The Hadim lost his cool in the Council Chamber and the Sultan sacked him as much for rudeness as graft. That was back in 1544. Since then the Hadim has gone to his maker and Rustem finds himself in such grandeur and so securely entrenched that one can safely say that he is the lord of the world.

Hayreddin too has become food for the worms. He lies by the side of the religious college that he founded on the banks of the Bosporus. He bequeathed two hundred slaves to Rustem, also writing off a prior loan of thirty thousand ducats, doubtless from a desire to win the Grand Vizier's sympathy for his heir Hassan, Governor of Algiers.

When you are admitted to Rustem's presence, which is easier to arrange than you might think, for he receives petitioners at home every day except Friday, you find a sturdy little workaholic the colour of stewed beetroot and wearing a vest from his own looms in Bursa. And when you are done being underwhelmed you meet his eyes, full of ambition and business, eyes that see more than yours do.

Some men are born to spend. A child of the White Sea, blustery and sparkling, Ibrahim the Frank commissioned a triple-tiered helmet crown for the Sultan that was made in Venice and cost a shade less than the annual budget of Egypt.

Rustem the Bosnian, on the other hand, started life where the sun sinks behind oppressive peaks and the valleys are wandered by furtive spirits of the dark green forest. Forget helmet crowns, Rustem is such a penny-pincher that he sells off vegetables, roses and Indian violets from the Sultan's own garden and auctions every last horse, helmet and breastplate that is captured in war. The Janissaries hate him for cutting their pay. And yet one might argue that he serves Suleyman more effectively than Ibrahim did. The Favourite increased the Sultan's standing by spending his money. The Son-in-law achieves the same end by saving it.

~

The viziers all keep a religious teacher at home to lead the servants in the five daily prayers. Rustem offers the position in his palace overlooking the Horn to a young scholar but the salary is low and the applicant objects. 'I can easily find an old, greybearded teacher who will accept less,' Rustem tells him. 'That may be so,' the young man replies cleverly, 'but did you know that the greybeards of whom you speak are charlatans and so impious that they can easily be bribed to give false testimony in court?'

Disconcerted by this information, Rustem instructs the young man to gain the trust of some of these teachers and he gives him expensive clothes and money for the purpose. The teacher duly makes the acquaintance of some older versions of himself and flashes his aspers. Then he tells them that he needs their help to come into an inheritance and gives them a cash advance with a promise of more if they bear witness on his behalf.

It is well known that the testimony of one geriatric mullah is worth that of ten healthy laymen. When two of the greybeards appear in court and swear that they have known the young teacher for years and that he is the legitimate son of the deceased, the judge finds in his favour. The young teacher brings the greybeards to Rustem who instead of congratulating them has them seated on a donkey and paraded around the city, then has their mouths beaten to a bloody pulp, and finally has them chained and sent to the galleys. And as a reward for a successful sting he agrees to pay the young man the salary he desires.

~

In a typical day he might seize the assets of wholesalers who have been buying up Turkish lentils and exporting them to the Christian market, order Ferdinand's man Malvezzi to be thrown into the Black Tower for his master's violations of the truce, and pocket two thousand florins from a certain judge in return for a desired appointment. When he tells Bernardo Navagero, the Venetian ambassador, 'I am a friend of the Signoria, but she does not know me and will only know me when she loses me,' the envoy takes the hint and advises the government back home to send the Grand Vizier 'reverently ... either cloth or choice silk ... for his and [Mihrimah's] clothing.' Rustem's love for his wife is perhaps his only redeeming feature.

Back when he was a junior vizier an earlier Hapsburg envoy mislaid a servant in Constantinople. Abducted by government agents, the servant was taken to a small room in the Covered Market where he was interrogated and beheaded. When the diplomat protested to Rustem he burst out laughing and asked, 'what will you do when many thousands are slain among you if you torture yourself so much over one man?'

Yes, he has other things to worry about than the little people. His brother, for instance, yet another Sinan, whose promotion to Captain Pasha he engineered despite the fact that Sinan's maritime experience was minimal, even for a Bosnian. His private investments which include villages, arable farms, workshops, tanneries, bakeries, one hundred and fifty-seven mills, eleven water wheels, more than five hundred and sixty shops, two hundred and seventy-three rooms for rent, fifty-four warehouses, fifteen commercial caravanserais, thirty-two commercial bathhouses and the Bursa looms. The prayer halls, schools of religious science, convents, caravanserais offering free rooms, public fountains, paved roads and toll-free bridges that make up his philanthropic portfolio. The land, black cattle and water buffaloes he receives from a mining contractor in lieu of tax on the gold he brings out of the ground.

He won't repeat Ibrahim the Frank's mistake of adding the suffix 'Sultan' to his title of commander-in-chief, which put the wind up the real Sultan. He won't brag to the ambassadors that he holds the reins. In truth he's already in a stronger position than Ibrahim was because the Frank's power rested solely on the love that the Sultan bore for him. Friendship blows hot and cold while a son-in-law is for life.

Another thing that marks him out from the Frank is that he is an observant Muslim who shuns alcohol. Perhaps he is atoning for his past intimacy with pigs, for did not the Prophet Solomon declare the pig to be the vilest of creatures?

Malvezzi considers Rustem to be a 'malignant perfidious dog who keeps the [Sultan's] whole court in a state of suffocation and does not allow anything to reach the Sultan's ears'. It's the old story of the 'just lord', in Malvezzi's words, who is kept 'blind' by his malevolent councillor. Not that the Sultan seems unhappy with his work–life balance which allows him to go boating with Cihangir, pursue his religious studies under the Mufti and enjoy the seasons at Edirne, where, in the words of the Venetian ambassador, 'once past the threshold he is among animals and in the light'.

~

The old Suleyman – the warrior, the sensualist, the lover – is exiting the scene. The new Suleyman is the ascetic, the sage, the lawgiver.

He has, Navagero writes, 'a marvellous greatness in his face with a sweetness that is agreeable to all who see him. He is very sober in what he eats, eating meat rarely and sparingly, and then only the red flesh of kids. No longer does he drink wine as he did in the time of Ibrahim, but a soft water,' and he is 'mindful of his infirmities ... the first being gout and the second a disposition to dropsy. He aspires to be very just ... as much as anybody of his dynasty he is a servant of his faith and his law and it is said that he has studied and wishes particularly to understand religious doctrine in order not to be found wanting in his word or his faith.'

His caftans of gorgeous crimson embroidered with gold thread and dripping with sapphires are back in the closet. Late-phase Suleyman favours humble robes of wool or cotton. One day he orders the gemstones and sheet gold with which the Frank covered the New Palace to be stripped from the walls. He has all the musical instruments in the palace burned. His pleasures consist of giving in to Mihrimah when she requests more money, letting little Huma Shah nuzzle into the strands of his beard, which he recently let grow out like a saint, and speaking to Ebussuud, with whom he is on terms of endearment, addressing him as 'my peer and my friend in the afterlife,' about their shared love of justice.

~

No sultanic law or *kanun* may challenge the sharia. But the sharia is silent on many things. Hence the need for *kanuns* on matters such as the tithes payable by a peasant who leaves his tenement in order to cultivate another tenement elsewhere, the correct sanction for forgery and the obligations of beekeepers. These *kanuns* are brought together in compilations known as law-books and are applied, with allowances for local tradition, across the Empire.

The practice was begun by Suleyman's grandfather Sultan Bayezit. On the honey question there were endless disputes over whether the hive-owner must pay his tithe to his fief-holder or to the owner of the meadow where the hives were positioned. A *kanun* issued by Bayezit stipulated that 'the tax should be set at two aspers per hive. The fief-holder of the place where the peasant is registered should take one asper, and the holder of the land where the hive produces honey should take one.'

Since then the Empire has tripled in size and more compilations are needed to introduce Ottoman law to the Sultan's new subjects. It falls to Ebussuud to find solutions to cases on which Hanafi law is ambiguous, standardise rules for the appointment of judges and produce templates for legal documents. And this work in progress is subject to constant review by the ruler who insists that it is royal justice which determines the welfare of the people, the amplitude of the treasury and the success of the army.

A good law doesn't break, only bends. A law which says that a peasant who leaves his field fallow for three successive years may be expelled by his landlord, for example, is a law worth adopting in spite of its origins in pagan Rome. Under earlier regimes the pig-drivers of Sofia were obliged to present a joint of pork to their lord at Christmas. Suleyman's law-books commute that to one asper per pair of swine, nor does he forego the old tax on wine, renaming it a tax on grape juice. In certain cities gypsy women who won't be deterred from perpetrating acts 'contrary to the sharia' are levied a fixed fine of one hundred aspers per month. It's less drastic than cutting them up and makes the government some money.

For all their detailed statutes, the law-letters were silent on basic principles until the province of Buda was created in 1541. All moveable goods, ran the first fiscal survey of that province, and all immovable goods which are above the ground, such as buildings, orchards and vineyards, are the property of their owners who may dispose of them as they wish. And who owns the land itself? 'The Muslim Treasury,' answers Ebussuud. And at a stroke of the pen of the Caliph of the Messenger of the Lord of the Worlds and the One who Makes Smooth the Path for the Precepts of the Manifest Sharia, as the mufti refers to his friend in the afterlife whenever he wishes to emphasise his function as a lawgiver, becomes the owner of all he surveys.

Suleyman of all people must not deviate from the law he embodies. He sees the logical conclusion of this embodiment, no matter how embarrassing it may be to the timeservers on the bench. Imagine the clearing of throats when one day he instructs the army judges, 'if my hand has to be cut according to religious law, do not hesitate to do so!'

~

Having remained in Edirne for the duration of the Iran campaign, Selim refuses to go back to Manisa. He and his mother appear to be of one mind, her commitment to his cause reinforced by the gifts that he lavishes on her. A meeting between father and son ends with a furious Suleyman, who would dearly love to be neutral in the matter of the succession, chasing Selim 'from his side with many threats and insults and calling him a disobedient son'.

It isn't in the cabal's interest for the Sultan to do something rash. The only beneficiary of Selim's death would be Mustafa. Enter Rustem the peacemaker who after vainly begging the errant prince for an audience, sends Suleyman a fictitious report claiming that the boy is contrite but too frightened to come forward. The Sultan's anger evaporates as it always does and he allows Selim to stay a little longer in Edirne, which defuses the crisis but may be storing up trouble for later.

In April 1550 Ferdinand's man Malvezzi reports that on the urging of the cabal the Sultan has removed Prince Bayezit from Konya and posted him to Kutahya, which is closer to Istanbul, a sign that the cabal may in fact be cooling on Selim and warming to Bayezit, which would make sense given that Selim is a drunk and Bayezit a promising young person full of a different kind of spirit, not that either of them enjoys anything like the popularity of Prince Mustafa. To which must be added caveats about the perils of changing horse mid-race.

~

Hurrem may not have been inactive during Suleyman's absence in Iran. It is reported that she and Mihrimah sent a man to the younger Sigismund of Poland, brother of Isabella of Transylvania for whom they have such affection, offering to intercede with the Sultan on Poland's behalf, and that Sigismund gave an honoured present to the messenger. When Rustem asks his wife if she sent an envoy to Poland, she says no, and Rustem, for once, is at a loss, wondering if the rumours were spread out of malice.

Reports, reports. The Sultan and Rustem aren't talking. The Sultan is dead. No he isn't. He has a bunion. And with each new sign that Suleyman isn't infallible or immune, but a man, and that his son-in-law is leading him with a ring through his nose, the aura gets a little weaker, a little frailer, a little nobler. Decline is all the more pathetic when state dogma insists that the wreck on the bed is surpassed only by God in potency and honour.

Would it not be preferable if the Ottoman system of government made allowance for the Sultan to shuffle off to Dimetoka and sit in his woollens cooing at his wife or expiate his geriatric bloodlust on the unsuspecting fauna of that well-endowed quarter? Is not this, or something like it, the exit that Charles V is said to be contemplating, his brother Ferdinand waiting for him to abdicate and retire to a monastery where he will kneel to negotiate with his future landlord? Not a drop of blood was shed when Henry succeeded Francis as Most Christian King, the retribution he exacted on Madame d'Etampes amounting to nothing more than the withdrawal of some jewels and a grace-and-favour apartment or two. But no, here in Turkey whenever the Sultan falls from his horse or cricks his neck there are terrible visions of a bloodbath of brothers and armies on the move. And at each false alarm the Christians and Jews nervously whittle up defensive weapons in readiness for the day when the Sultan's enraged and grief-stricken subjects round on the minorities for no other reason than that they can.

Weakness is about perception, at least to begin with. Then weakness catches up. Sultan Bayezit, that ruler of saintly rather than warlike character, was doomed from the moment three of his sons, Ahmet, Korkut and Selim, decided that each of them must pre-empt his brothers and seize the throne. In the event it was Selim who got to the New Palace first, in April 1512, sending his father away to retirement but in reality to his death.

XIV

Transylvania is the richest region of Hungary, bringing in enormous revenue from silver, salt, lumber and horses, and from Transylvania it is easy to seize the rest of Hungary while the opposite is not the case. So observes Ferdinand in a letter to Charles, adding that 'should the Turk recover [Transylvania] . . . I will deserve certain condemnation.' Ferdinand bases his claim to Hungary on a secret agreement he reached with Janos back in 1538 under which the kingdom would devolve to the House of Austria following Janos's death. From a Turkish point of view Hungary was conquered fair and square at the Battle of Mohacs and is being kept warm for young John Sigismund.

Queen Isabella and Brother George Martinuzzi have been tetchily cohabiting ever since the Sultan exiled them from Buda in 1541, they and John Sigismund who will soon enough be a man. The Ottoman pashas and tributaries whose lands lie to the east, south and west of the principality have orders to favour the Queen. To the north is territory belonging to Ferdinand who is urging Brother George to implement the agreement of '38. And Brother George can pretty much do as he wants, for he is the principality's commander-in-chief, treasurer and chief justice.

When relations between George and Isabella were more amicable he gave a banquet and after dinner a troupe of musicians got the guests to their feet. The dowager danced with the monk, whose moves were admired by all, the guests also contrasting Isabella's elegance while dancing in a demure hood with the conduct of her ladies who, when they were not vomiting, which they did with alarming frequency, danced hoodless.

She has her castles, he has his. But all state income goes through him and she must make do with the bare necessities, a great privation for the favourite daughter of the King of Poland who grew up under coffered ceilings and surrounded by Italian art in the royal residence at Krakow. Complaining that she is as much a prisoner in Transylvania as she was during the siege of Buda, she tells the Sultan in a letter that the person whom 'your Serenity deputed to govern our realm has ... committed many thefts and ... has taken for himself all the revenues leaving nothing to eat.' 'Of the riches he has extracted,' she goes on slyly, 'he has sent little to your Serenity, sending the entire Treasury to [Ferdinand].'

In 1550 the Sultan gives orders that Brother George is to be replaced by one of Isabella's allies but the monk lays siege to the Queen at the provincial capital, Alba Iulia. Isabella begs the Turks to send troops, then changes her mind and when the Pasha of Buda arrives with his army he finds Brother George forewarned, and the Pasha is put to flight. The following spring Ferdinand sends a multinational force led by one of his brother's most experienced soldiers, Giovanni Battista Castaldo, with orders to implement the 1538 agreement and oversee the handover of Transylvania to Austria.

Brother George is thought to prefer the Austrians to the Turks as the lesser of two evils, but did he not lead the defence against Roggendorf in Buda in '41, facilitating the Sultan's annexation of the city? Nor is it clear where his personal ambitions lie. The path from mastery of Transylvania to the throne of Hungary has been trodden before.

'The time has come,' he tells the Queen on bended knee at their next meeting, 'that Transylvania and the crown of Hungary be handed over to Ferdinand.' On the subject of her religious obligations, he goes on, 'Christian princes turn their eyes to you. Your memory would be an abomination to them if you preferred the protection of the Turkish Emperor to that of the King of the Romans.' And the Queen bursts into tears.

On 19 July 1551 Isabella surrenders Transylvania and her late husband's share of the Hungarian Kingdom to Ferdinand in return for the Duchy of Oppeln in Upper Silesia, which is closer to Krakow than it is to Alba Iulia. At an assembly of nobles Brother George asks her to hand over the crown of St Stephen, the sacred crown upon which the strength and liberty of the realm are based, but she replies that she will not make a friar a king and gives it to Castaldo to pass on to his master.

The first time she went into exile it was at the behest of a king to wed another king. Two years later the king of Turkey expelled her from Buda. Now a fourth king is sending her away from Transylvania. She is thirty-two years of age and has had her fill of kings, except for her son at her side who is a king but not yet a king! Isabella's anguish diminishes not one scintilla as her coach struggles over the rugged mountains which divide Transylvania from the plain, and ascending a steep ridge she is obliged to get out and continue on foot, accompanied by her ladies, the dancing and vomiting no more than fond memories, and as she trudges through the mud and rain she laments her iniquitous destiny, which, not content with assailing her with great misfortunes, now wishes to afflict her with small ones. Taking up a knife, with its sharp point she scratches into the bark of a great tree, under which she has taken refuge from the incessant rain, the words SIC FATA VOLUNT, Such is the will of the fates, and below that, ISABELLA REGINA.

~

Giovanni Battista Castaldo achieved fame at the Battle of Pavia, the first of King Francis's abortive attempts to seize Milan from the Emperor. As the cream of French nobility lay dying, it fell to the young cavalry officer to take Francis into captivity, an honour that also brought him Francis's golden crown which he converted into a necklace. Now pushing sixty, Castaldo has devoted himself to Charles's service and was recently awarded two Italian countships in recognition of his contribution to the victory over the Lutherans at Muhlberg.

The force he has brought to Transylvania comprises seven thousand four hundred Spanish, German, Italian and Bohemian troops. Too big for an embassy, as the saying goes, too small for an army. Brother George ingratiates himself with his well-connected guest, mentioning in passing that he wouldn't say no to a cardinal's hat, but he is also trying to appease the Sultan who is angry that his property has been stolen and his protégés turfed out. Among the sweeteners he sends the Porte are an offer to increase the annual tribute and a promise to drive away the Hapsburgs, not that it is clear how he will achieve the latter. As Malvezzi notes from his cell overlooking the Bosporus, 'Brother George is a rogue and an evil hypocrite who pulls out one of his own eyes to take both his neighbour's.'

In another life this monk from the Balkans might have been included in the boy levy and ended up a second Rustem. He does not see the Turks in stark or rhetorical terms, as Luther did and many Popes have done, but as a problem to solve in all its complexity and threat. Has he not warned Ferdinand that the Turks are luring the people of Hungary towards Islam, urging him to emancipate the oppressed peasants 'that they might know of his Majesty's concern for all the estates and classes of his realm'? And yet duplicity is a condition of survival in the borderlands between Islam and Christendom. Which leaves Giovanni Battista Castaldo, that blunt and straightforward man of action, to puzzle over the monk's nature, 'which is . . . to argue first for, then against, and in doing so to leave everyone else irresolute, thus gaining time while he waits patiently for the opportunity he seeks.'

On 7 September 1551 an Ottoman army under Mehmet Sokollu, Governor of Rumelia, crosses the Danube with retribution in mind. Brother George rouses the people in the traditional way, which is to say that a knight, showing off a bloodied sword and lance, goes from town to town accompanied by a man on foot who shouts, 'the enemy of the fatherland is approaching, let every home send its man to save us from the common danger!'

Advancing eastwards, Sokollu seizes Christian strongholds culminating in the capture of Lipova, on the left bank of the Mures, where in times of peace the boats are loaded with Transylvanian salt for export. Leaving behind a garrison of five thousand horsemen and two hundred Janissaries, he takes the rest of his soldiers back to Belgrade for the winter and on 5 November a joint force led by Castaldo and Brother George opens the siege of Lipova with a ferocious bombardment.

Cardinal Martinuzzi, as we must now call him, a courier from Rome having brought the glad tidings a few days ago, wears a green cloak over his habit to prevent recognition by the enemy, and he gives heart to all as he did at Buda ten years ago, only this time for the other side. And when the smoke clears and twelve hundred Turks lie dead, Lipova is overrun.

Some of the surviving Turks gallop away but only as far as the cavalry that Castaldo has positioned on the Mures for this very reason, those not immediately cut down being dispatched by the Spaniards and Bohemians who await them on the opposite bank. The rest flee to the fortress above the town and, such is their terror and confusion, many men fall to their deaths in the ditch below. Then a second siege begins whose weapons are hunger and thirst. By 18 November the defenders have been reduced to eating cats and horses and drinking their horses' blood.

The Ottoman commander is an Iranian defector called Ulama Bey. He sends word that he wishes to negotiate the fortress's surrender in return for safe passage for him and his men. And Brother George sees in Ulama's offer a chance to appease the Sultan.

'Gentlemen,' he says, addressing the assembled Hapsburg and Transylvanian captains, 'I believe that you understand and know how tremendous the force of the Great Lord is, and how great his power.' By 'Great Lord' he means Suleyman. Rather than provoke him further by starving or slaughtering the besieged army, 'one must explore every avenue to placate him and render him benevolent and clement.' These are the words of a man who is thinking about the day after and they are well received by the Transylvanians, who realise that they will bear the brunt of Turkish retribution.

Not, however, by Castaldo. 'What drives and motivates soldiers to war,' he asks bitterly, 'if not the goal of glory, and of acquiring honour, fame, and rewards through endeavour, and now that you have ... gained these things, and put an end to this war, do you want, to your great shame and detriment, to hand triumph to your enemies?'

Castaldo too is thinking of the day after. 'What will be said among Christians if not that you were frightened at seeing the Turks in your power, that you immediately fled, that you hadn't the courage to imprison them?' And turning to the Transylvanian nobles, he says, 'don't you also realise ... that it will be the Spaniards, Germans and Bohemians who will receive the palm for having defeated them, and you the infamy for having let them go?'

Brother George replies coldly that he intends to let Ulama go in order to bring peace to Transylvania and assure the wellbeing of its people. And he sends Ulama an offer of safe conduct, also extracting from Castaldo an undertaking that his soldiers will not molest the enemy as they depart.

On 5 December, a moonlit night, Ulama and his men come out of the citadel in proud defiance, armed, mounted and well-fed, having been sent provisions by Brother George, also equipped with carts for the wounded and a guard of one thousand Serbs as protection against Castaldo. Before Ulama sets out for Belgrade, the Cardinal receives him in his tent and they speak for four hours, perhaps about their shared experience of changing sides, and to show his gratitude Ulama gives him a gold lamp, two gilded tapers, a richly embroidered Persian shawl, a bejewelled dagger and four war horses. Castaldo, who once captured the King of France, can only watch.

Later on Castaldo's men do in fact ambush Ulama, who gives a good account of himself and makes it back to Belgrade, though not without sustaining more casualties. Castaldo tells Ferdinand that Martinuzzi's frequent communications with the Turks are designed less to forestall a large-scale invasion than to encourage one. And Ferdinand replies that an end must be put to the intrigues of the monk.

~

On 13 December Castaldo and Brother George travel in a coach along the valley of the Mures to the latter's castle seven miles south-west of Alba Iulia. While Brother George prepares for a forthcoming diet of Transylvanian nobles, Castaldo confers secretly with another Italian commander of long service, Sforza Pallavicino. 'I have led the Cardinal to this castle,' Castaldo tells Pallavicino, 'and I do not wish him to leave it alive.' That evening Brother George attends Mass in the course of which the priest drops the chalice containing the wine of the Sacrament but the Cardinal pays no heed to this augury of blood to come.

Over the next few days Spanish soldiers slip into the castle and hide in the towers and the principal assassins are allotted their roles, notably the Cardinal's secretary, Marc Antonio Ferrari. On 16 December an unsuspecting Brother George sends his bodyguard of two hundred men to Alba Iulia, he himself intending to follow on the next morning.

That night the sky is especially dark, as if it wishes to give some notice, and there is a tempest the like of which no one who witnesses it can remember, with such a rattling of doors and windows that they are nearly forced from their frames and one would believe that all the devils and sprites are in a frenzy to get in. And at daybreak Pallavicino and his devils get to work.

Shortly after dawn Ferrari approaches his master's chamber whose door is unlocked and unguarded. Whether it is because he remembers the gifts and affectionate caresses that he has received from the old man, or because he is thinking ahead to the verdict of God, Ferrari hesitates before crossing the threshold. Behind him stands Sforza Pallavicino who, noting his unease, shoves him into the room while keeping the door ajar.

The Cardinal is in a fur-lined robe against the cold and bent over a writing table on which stands a clock, a breviary, a diary and an inkstand. He nods to Ferrari to come forward and the younger man places some papers on the table, adding that Pallavicino is leaving for Vienna and wishes to kiss the hand of His Eminence and to know if he has orders for him.

As Martinuzzi takes up his pen, Ferrari draws his dagger and stabs him twice, once in the chest and once in the neck. Martinuzzi cries out, 'Lord! Why are you doing this to me?' He touches his hand to his wound which seems to enrage him for belying his seventy years he seizes Ferrari and hurls him to the floor. Pallavicino rushes into the room with drawn sword and strikes Martinuzzi a violent blow to the head. Then the concealed Spaniards also enter at a run and discharge their arquebuses into the stricken man's chest.

For seventy days his body lies frozen and untouched in the room where he fell until Archduke Ferdinand gives permission for it to be removed to Alba Iulia and interred in the cathedral church. Not that his death much avails the Hapsburgs for along with the Cardinal is well and truly buried the truce of '47. In 1552 the Sultan's armies rampage through Hungary capturing twenty-five strongholds while the Turkish fleet ravages the coasts of southern Italy and causes the people of Naples to flee, Rustem's brother Sinan picking up where Barbarossa left off.

Act Five: The Bow

XV

King Francis, Martin Luther, Pope Paul. Infidels he has buried. Along with friends like the Hadim and Hayreddin. Not that longevity means much if the time is squandered. Sultan Selim died ruing that he hadn't dealt properly with the red-headed ones, waged holy war against Christendom or built himself a memorial mosque.

Shortly before setting out on his recent Iran campaign, 'his Highness the world-ruling Sultan realised the impermanence of the base world . . . and the necessity of leaving behind a monument so as to be commemorated till the end of time and to rejoice with the grateful remembrance of pious deeds.' So writes the chronicler.

Mosque building is about many things. The common purpose of dome and pillar. The grain of the stone and the uniformity of the tiles, the purity of their whites and the luminosity of their reds. Above all it is about cubit envy.

Aya Sofya is sixty-nine cubits from one side of its slightly elliptical drum to the other. No Ottoman mosque comes close. So when Suleyman melts down his tableware and mints one hundred and fifty thousand gold coins to get the ball rolling, when Sinan shows him his plans for the complex with its five theological colleges, hospice, guest house, hospital, gardens, graveyards and mausolea, the site in its totality encompassing an area the size of the Hungarian city of Pressburg; when on

27 June 1549 he goes to the Third Hill with its prospect over the Horn and lays the foundation stone with his own blessed hands and the chief architect occupies a room on the noble site from which he emerges, his prayer beads in his right hand and his measuring stick in his left, to scold and assail negligent master-craftsmen – in short, when the Sultan builds himself a memorial mosque, it has a lot to do with swinging dicks.

~

Under the Mamluks Jerusalem was sacked by Bedouins and its inhabitants were driven away by drought. Early in his reign Suleyman rebuilt the walls that encircle the city, also giving it an aqueduct, a reservoir and drinking fountains whose inscriptions refer to him as a second Solomon and his wife as the Queen of Sheba. Now the pilgrims, guides, hostel-keepers and peddlers of soap and olive oil have returned, supplemented by Jewish refugees from Hapsburg persecution. The Sultan is currently restoring and embellishing the Noble Sanctuary which contains the mosque of al-Aqsa and the Dome of the Rock, the rock in question being the Prophet's port of embarkation when he made his night journey to heaven.

The Haseki's Palestinian endowments include land and villages in Nablus, Gaza, Safad and Sidon, as well as urban property in Tripoli and Jericho. In Jerusalem she is converting the palace of Tunshuq al-Muzaffariyya, an earlier slave girl whose fortunes looked up, into a hostel for fifty-five residents. Encroaching into a knot of streets known as the Lady's Quarter, perhaps because Queen Helena, mother of Emperor Constantine, built a hospice for pilgrims here, the completed complex will boast a mosque, soup kitchen, bakery and Quran school for orphans. An irregular leggy thing that wraps itself around the old city, not one of Sinan's paragons of symmetry and proportion! But it's what happens inside that interests God and this will include prayers according to the Hanafi rite and free food and lodging for the poor.

Her husband recently increased her stipend to two thousand

aspers a day, ten times the sum his mother received. And so rich and committed a philanthropist has Hurrem become that whenever she learns of a place in need of assistance she orders her fortune to be spent on it, building Friday mosques and convents for sheikhs and constructing religious schools for the doctors of the law. If she hears about a dilapidated prayer hall, she has it repaired, and builds countless new ones as well as waterworks and bridges. She builds reservoirs at waystations on the road to Holy Mecca and a conduit to bring water to the Kaaba, God's house. A hospice in the same city bears her name and one in Medina is under construction.

For the pilgrims she provides travelling provisions, including saddled horses and medicines. She endows funds for soldiers who have been separated from their baggage while campaigning and gives weapons and horses to holy warriors on the frontiers. She commissions scribes to write books of excellence for distribution to students throughout the Empire's protected domains and if she hears of a rare curiosity she takes pains to bring it to Istanbul. For instance she has imported a golden goblet from the island of Kos, multi-layered velvets from Europe and from Egypt a thousand pairs of Yusufi turtledoves for use as mail pigeons.

It's all about the giving, of course, but while the Haseki ensures celebrity for herself in this world and bliss in the next, while she promotes herself as the Zubayda of the age, her rival Mahidevran is treading water in the provinces without so much as a public fountain to her name. Surely that will count for something in the court of public opinion?

~

Amasya is known for its orchards. It lies inland from the Black Sea between the historic regions of Cappadocia and Greater Armenia, its houses, mosques and other buildings arranged along the steep banks of the Yesilirmak. Iran is twenty days away, Istanbul about the same. An in-between place, near nowhere, a cage for a prince.

On the town's eastern elevation, behind a wooden gate framed in mud, single-storey buildings of rough-cut boards and fired bricks accommodate a harem, state rooms, kitchens and bathhouses. There is a tower made of wood and an arbour covered with shingles. The buildings are not without cracks and other signs of damage caused by the earthquakes that are a frequent occurrence.

This royal residence was built a century and a half ago by Prince Mehmet, who went on to become the fifth Ottoman Sultan and should not be confused with his grandson Mehmet the Conqueror or our own recently deceased Prince Mehmet. Its other distinction is that it is the birthplace of Sultan Selim.

Mustafa looks like his father. The same slim build, the same swan-like neck and swallow-wing moustaches, the Prince's face perhaps a little squarer, the nose a little less aquiline. Mahidevran runs his household in Amasya as she did the one in Manisa. She is in her early fifties. A certain Mustafa Efendi shadows his namesake in his capacity as the royal tutor. Not that the Prince, in his mid thirties, has many educational gaps to fill but he is obliged to let the Efendi discharge the unwritten provision of his royal appointment which is to spy on him and report what he does.

Besides administering the province of Amasya, overseeing the development of his son Mehmet and lavishing gifts on favoured poets who repay his generosity by writing odes in the violet, rosebud or tulip metre, there isn't much to do. The irony is that a born warrior and leader of men is confined to barracks and his small army relegated to fire-fighting duties. Mustafa's most recent plan to march against the Georgians was squashed by Rustem on the grounds, unsaid but apparent to all, that the Prince must not be allowed to raise his public profile through acts of military valour.

There's a precedent to guard against. In 1508, when Selim was little older than Mustafa is now, and governing Trabzon for his father Sultan Bayezit, he led an army into Georgia where, according to the authorised biographer, the accursed people of that land were scattered and enslaved and Selim's men ended up 'spoil-laden and satiated through looting and plundering'. Facing his troops Selim delivered his first stump speech for the sultanate, denouncing the 'incompetent people, the purse-snatchers, the men greedy for wealth and possessions' who monopolised his father's court, also promising high positions to the 'capable and distinguished, sword-wielding champion war-riors' standing in front of him. Four years later came the New Palace coup and the debacle of Dimetoka.

Mahidevran protects him from every mishap, reminding him constantly that he has nothing to fear but being poisoned, and that he need only wait and the Janissaries will hand him the sul-tanate after his father dies. And for all the lack of philanthropic endowments in her name she can console herself that the char-ity dispensed by the Haseki has failed to win her the love of her husband's subjects. They do not call her Zubayda or the Queen of Sheba. They call her 'witch'. And then there is the hatred that the people feel for Hurrem's son-in-law on account of his ridicu-lous callousness and tightfistedness.

Rustem's recent transactions include the receipt of eighty thousand aspers from Ulama Pasha, the same Iranian turncoat who eluded Castaldo at Lipova. Much of his own income he somehow omits to declare. The Grand Vizier's lucrative side-hustle is farming out the tax. And yet this same man who when going home has three palaces to choose from finds it within himself to annul a sainted and noble scheme, started by Sultan Bayezit, under which the poor receive four aspers to buy broad-cloth or a cape to keep off the rain. A vault in the Treasury which is so full of coins that no more can be crammed in bears the inscription, 'money accumulated by the care of Rustem'. For 'care' might one not substitute 'spite' or 'meanness'?

Yes, when the time comes the Grand Vizier's head will be first on the block. And as if Prince Mustafa wishes to demonstrate how different his regime will be from the current one, each day the doors of his residence open to receive generous quantities of meat, oil, suet, rice, honey, grape juice, almonds, molasses and so on, the better to regale any passing Janissary or government official. Mustafa does not confine himself to the red meat of kids, he enjoys a glass or two from the fruit of the vineyards that Amasya's landowners have given him in recognition of his just and benevolent rule. So confident is he in his standing, so settled in his culture, that when a local scholar, Kemaleddin, castigates him in a book for spending too much and even dares to send him a copy, rather than furrow his brow, far less imprison his critic, Mustafa gives Kemaleddin a reward!

The winters here are perishing but the apples are everything they say they are. And the news from Edirne is that the Sultan is fading. It won't be long now.

~

Suleyman's soldiers fight in Hungary and his sailors on the White Sea while he writhes on his bed in Thrace. In the winter of 1551 Shah Tahmasp, who has many spies and exploits any distraction, hesitation or discord in the Sultan's realms, enters through the back door.

Dividing his horsemen into four columns, he orders one to Ardahan, hard by the Georgian mountains, one, commanded by his son Ismail, to Erzurum and another to Mesopotamia while he himself leads the fourth to Lake Van. At Ahlat on the northern shore he taunts the besieged townsfolk saying that the Sultan is far away and the pashas are occupied fighting the Austrians, urging them not to waste their breath for no one will hear their cries for help. Then he offers them safe passage which must be his idea of a joke for as soon as they surrender he puts them to the sword, women and children included. From Ahlat the Iranians come away with thirty thousand sheep, three thousand horses and ten thousand head of cattle and water buffalo.

Since the Sultan's last inconclusive eastern campaign, Iskender Pasha, the Governor of Erzurum, has raided the lands of the Shah, burning the bazaar at Yerevan and ordering three Ottoman district governors to build a fortress in Safavid territory.

Young Ismail and his army of fifteen thousand horse destroy the uncompleted fortress and the commanders are dispatched by fraction, one being roasted whole, a second sawn in half and a third quartered. Then, turning their backs on Mount Ararat, where Noah's ark came to rest, the Iranians ride to the fortress of Erzurum which Iskender is defending with a skeleton force.

From his concealed position half a farsakh from the city Ismail sends a small squad under the walls intending Iskender to believe that this is his total strength. And Iskender rises like one of the Shah's brown trout, he and his men galloping out of the citadel and into Ismail's trap. Now the Turks are surrounded by a force incomparably larger than their own. Among the few survivors is Iskender himself, who manages to scale his own walls, severely wounded, before the Iranians race away to their next target.

Bitlis. Ercis. Kars. Nowhere is safe in the hard, white, treeless back end of Asia Minor. Further south a belt of Ottoman Mesopotamia eight days' march in width and thirty in length is obliterated by the Iranians who operate with the delicacy of locusts. And in the spring of 1553 the Shah and his men, spoil-laden and satiated, retire eastwards to their summer quarters on the Nakhchivan River.

'May your face be blemishless in this world and the next,' the Sultan writes to Iskender. 'You did not have the measure of the army of the Shah's son but you stood your ground and lacked nothing in heroism. Who wins and loses depends on the will of God.' And he sends him a ceremonial caftan, gilded sword and ornamented mace.

Suleyman has never been jealous of his power, never hoarded it or exercised it arbitrarily, the way his father did. He appoints people and lets them get on with it. If the Governor of Erzurum suffers defeat through an excess of zeal he is not executed, which would be the action of a tyrant, but consoled and transferred. And so, through the Sultan's example, his appointments and his laws, spreads the arch of justice. From Buda to Basra, Crimea to North Africa, Ottoman governors and judges are told to strengthen and buttress the arch. Is this not the meaning of empire?

And is it not a tragedy, greater even than that witnessed under the walls of Erzurum, that Prince Mustafa has inside him something of Suleyman's spirit? That he, more than any of his brothers, is his father's son?

~

In the autumn of 1552 Suleyman orders his Second Vizier to Hungary to secure his rear. He sends the Army of Rumelia to central Anatolia to prepare for the spring offensive against Iran, also dispatching Rustem, in his new capacity as commander-in-chief, eastwards at the head of fifty thousand men. The governors-general, provincial governors, district governors and fief-holders receive orders to prepare their men for war. All three Janissary divisions muster in central Anatolia.

It's a panache in Rustem's turban to have attained the same military rank as Ibrahim did. That said, now may not be the best time to be putting half a continent between him and his master. Back in 1520, when Sultan Selim died on the road from Edirne to Istanbul, the Grand Vizier, Piri Pasha, was at his side. Piri summoned Prince Suleyman from Manisa while he oversaw the body's transfer to the capital under the guise of a remittance of imperial coin. The Grand Vizier himself rode ahead incognito to forestall any disruption on the part of the Janissaries. Not that they had any reason to interfere with this particular succession, Suleyman being the sole candidate on a shortlist of one, but when have the Janissaries ever needed an excuse to tip over their cauldrons and go on a spree?

That the transfer of power of 1520 went so smoothly can be attributed to the foresight of the late Sultan who had trimmed the shortlist in his inimitable manner. Piri's proximity to his master when the latter expired made it one for the training manuals. The succession that is now about to unfold, by contrast, will be complex. A shortlist of three; the cabal and the Janissaries at odds; the Sultan on the fence. Also, there's no way of knowing which candidate will get early news of the Sultan's death, whether they will act pre-emptively, or where the Janissaries will be when the time comes.

The last thing the cabal wants is for Rustem to be hundreds of miles away when he should be at the seat of government playing the Piri role to perfection. Nor would it be advisable for him to be stranded among thousands of hostile Janissaries when his father-in-law breathes his last. So it isn't surprising that when he leads his men into Asia Minor in the autumn of 1552 it isn't with the speed we have come to expect from an Ottoman army on the move. Far from achieving the seven farsakhs a day of which he should be capable – more, if he marches through the night under flares – he drags his feet and blames the snow. Come mid November, a full two months after setting out from Istanbul, he hasn't even reached Konya.

Two days shy of that felicitous city the road forks, one prong heading into town before skirting the Anti-Taurus by way of its southern foothills, the second looping around the same range to the north, into Cappadocia and on to Amasya. When they reach the fork, the Janissaries inform Rustem that they intend to divert along the northern route in order to pay their respects to their future sovereign. And when Rustem orders them not to do so they go ahead anyway.

At Amasya Mustafa feeds them up and gives each man a gold ducat for his pains, and the Janissaries address him with the following words. 'Your illustrious father is old, he is unable to campaign and is obliged to send the Grand Vizier as commander in his place. There is no doubt that if he had his way, he would step aside for you, but Rustem prevents this. If you cut off Rustem's head and take over the army, all the men will support you and the old Emperor can spend the rest of his days in prayer in Dimetoka, which he, being tired, will do in all happiness.'

Among Mustafa's advisers there is a slave of Venetian origin, a member of the noble house of Michiel, who was captured at the Battle of Prevesa while serving his apprenticeship on a galley, entered the Prince's service and perhaps now sees a role for himself under Sultan Mustafa I. An Alvise Gritti role, an Ibrahim the Frank role, without the nasty end. The Prince consults Michiel, his doctor of the law and Mahidevran. Above all he consults his own conscience and reaches his own conclusion.

To take arms against the Grand Vizier would be to take arms against the Sultan. It would be to risk a recurrence of that infamous scene back in 1512 when Selim and his men stormed the New Palace and, having slaughtered anyone standing in their way, overthrew Sultan Bayezit at sword-point. To rebel against the Caliph of Islam, against one's own father, would be a violation of the Sharia and a breach of morality for which this prince has no stomach. So Mustafa, still smiling, still thanking the Janissaries for their loyalty and assuring them that he will soon have great use for them, sends them back to join the main body of the army.

~

But the moment is approaching. It's coming on fast, isn't it? So hard to tell when the Sultan is dying one day and picking mushrooms the next. Work on his memorial mosque is advancing at such a pace that Sinan would appear to have orders to complete it as a matter of urgency. The Sultan recently made Sinan show him the exact place where he is to be buried, soothing the chief architect's agitation with the words, 'I know well that death is common to all and that I am old.'

In the summer of 1552 Mustafa writes to Ayas Pasha, not the long-dead Ayas Pasha of the forty cots but the newly appointed Governor of Erzurum. And Mustafa opens by noting with studied neutrality that 'in this transitory mansion no person is immortal' and that 'it is certain and decided that every soul will be separated from the body to which it is connected and return to its source'.

After his father's death, the Prince goes on, he intends 'within a few days' to take the sultanate on the basis of his superior talents and capabilities. And having done so he will distribute 'a variety of considerations and favours' to those 'viziers, commanders, large fief-holders, horsemen and all the victorious soldiers' who have helped him. This is a reference to Ayas and other men in high positions to whom he sends the same letter.

In his reply Ayas acclaims Mustafa as 'the most worthy and justified' of the candidates, a 'shining sun' to whom all incline, high and low, and he affirms that he is prepared to 'lay down sweet life at the foot of [your] exalted throne'. He also reminds the Prince not to forget him when it comes to giving out jobs.

Promise the earth but keep it vague. Mustafa needs no lessons in patronage. Or in shaping the narrative. His Venetian slave longs for news of his Michiel relations and that autumn Mustafa sends a state messenger to the Serenissima. The messenger passes on Prince Mustafa's greetings to the Doge. And the government of Venice makes a great fuss of him, hoping in this way to win the goodwill of the man who will become the eleventh Sultan of the Ottoman Empire.

~

The Sipahis or feudal cavalry are free-born Muslims. Their commanders are granted fiefs by the Sultan and they supply him men and mounts for war. Each Sipahi has a slave groom who spends hours brushing his horse and dyeing any white patches in the mane or tail with henna. The Sipahis disdain firearms, considering it ungentlemanly to kill an enemy by explosive means, and they get upset if their gorgeous clothes are scorched or speckled with gunpowder. The Sipahis hate the Janissaries, convert slaves who trudge around in the mud and shoot anything that moves. The Janissaries hate them back.

The commander of the Sipahis is Semsi Ahmet Pasha. He is the son of Sultan Selim's niece. Semsi Ahmet is known for his love of mushrooms, which Suleyman indulges, gathering them for him and preserving them in his handkerchief before handing them over with kind words. When the pair are out hunting Semsi refrains from going after a rabbit so as not to interrupt a story that his cousin is telling, and the Sultan, who is informed about this, praises his tact.

One day that winter Semsi Ahmet arrives unexpectedly at the New Palace. He is carrying a letter from Rustem in which the Grand Vizier informs the Sultan that the Janissaries are urging Prince Mustafa to overthrow him and that Prince Mustafa has raised the banner of rebellion.

A lie is more easily swallowed when it is mixed with a truth. All the same, the Sultan cannot bring himself to believe that 'while I live Mustafa should dare show such insolence'. Rather, he suspects that 'some seditious people' in the camp of Prince Selim or Prince Bayezit are 'spreading these calumnies', their objective being to provoke him to kill Mustafa and place the country 'into the hands of the prince they favour'. And, rounding on his cousin, who, as a Sipahi, can be expected to derive pleasure from any sign that the Janissaries have disgraced themselves, he growls, 'never again utter these words and do not allow such bad situations and evil to come to pass'.

In the same letter Rustem entreats the Sultan to take his rightful place at the head of his troops. Ibrahim sent him a similar plea years ago when he felt out of his depth on the Iranian frontier. Sooner or later everyone needs Daddy.

And it cannot be denied that Rustem is in danger. He is encamped with the army on a distant Anatolian plain and the tents are full of mutiny. The Sultan sends Semsi back with orders that the Janissaries are to break camp and return to Istanbul. He also instructs Rustem to come home. Next year this battered old warhorse will surprise the Janissaries who have put him out to pasture!

~

She sent Mustafa poison but the Prince was cautious, under the influence of his mother, and the poison was discovered before it could do harm. She brought her two candidates closer to Istanbul so that Suleyman's affection for them would grow. She reconciled her husband and son-in-law when they fell out over a slight.

A story that began with a slave ship in the Black Sea, the nails of Mahidevran tearing at her hair, her first erotic examination of the Sultan's long, swan-like neck. Who if not Hafsa of blessed memory impressed on her the necessity of forward planning? Twenty years of family-building, tactical alliances and attempted murder. Always working to the same objective, never letting it slip from view.

Yet even now her husband continues to profess impartiality and is resolved to abide by the decree of Mehmet the Conqueror and leave the rest to God.

Then another letter arrives. Mustafa has gone over to the Shah of Iran and will marry his daughter. That the claim is a lie is curiously immaterial. In the hothouse of suspicion false allegations and true ones prosper equally.

Armed with the new accusation the cabal go to work on Suleyman in their different ways, with kind words, tears, caresses, cajolings, threats and appeals to the bones of his ancestors.

And Suleyman, who is one against three, begins to doubt.

With his friend Ebussuud the Mufti he approaches the subject sideways. 'There is at Istanbul,' he remarks one day, 'a merchant of good position who, when about to leave for some time, placed over his property and household a slave to whom he had shown the greatest favour, and entrusted his wife and children to his loyalty. No sooner was the master gone than this slave began to embezzle his master's property, plot against the lives of his wife and children and attempt to compass his master's destruction. Answer me this: what sentence can be lawfully pronounced against him?'

~

As soon as it becomes public knowledge that the Sultan himself will lead a campaign against Iran, Shah Tahmasp hurriedly sends a negotiator with full powers. On 19 August the negotiator is admitted to the Imperial Council where he delivers a poem.

O exalted sovereign,
Highness Suleyman with the pomp of Alexander,
Whatever you command, leadership is yours,
For you to point, for us to obey.
Can a rift this deep be lawful?
What do you say to an accord between us?
If you would be kind enough to give your assent to peace,
We would send up prayers for you forever,
Accept our plea and our bow,
In the name of God and the name of the Prophet.

Hearken to the sound of a Shah shitting bricks.

~

On the sixteenth day of the month of Ramadan, which this year coincides with 28 August, the Janissary Corps stand outside the gate of the New Palace, all twelve thousand of them, each man with his white cap, his arquebus, his insurrectionary thoughts. Rustem is also present in a state of readiness.

When Suleyman rides through the gate he is accompanied by Cihangir. Perhaps because Prince Mustafa showed him kindness when he was a sickly boy in the Old Palace, Cihangir has much affection for his half-brother. And after Mustafa, Cihangir is the best-loved of the Sultan's children. As he rides past the soldiers they shout, 'God preserve you from mistakes and from manifold unseen perils.'

The musketeers fire salvo after salvo and across everyone goes to the Asian shore where the rest of the men are waiting. The army sets out in a south-easterly direction, an unusual feature of the march being the flock of vultures that follows overhead. Near Bursa the doctors of the law spot the new moon and proclaim the end of the fasting month.

After prayers the next morning the men receive their holiday bonuses and give themselves over to feasting. When they can eat no more a man comes forward with his hands tied behind him and saddles up a horse using his mouth, also putting on its bridle, stirrups and girth in the same way. Carrying a child on his shoulders he steps barefoot over the blades of scimitars and onto the horse. After dismounting he is put into a sack from which, using his teeth and his feet, he fires an arrow which cleanly passes through a bronze plaque two fingers wide. Another man comes forward with a hen egg which he swallows whole. Half an hour later he expels the egg from his arse breaking not the egg but plenty of wind. Then the men stagger about diffusing muttony smells and playing a game that involves a rope, a lot of pushing and a meeting of heels.

Another of Ebussuud's recent fatwas states that it is as meritorious to kill a Shia in war as it is to kill a Christian and that it is permitted to seize their possessions. But blood lust either comes naturally or not at all and as the Sultan resumes his march eastwards the Slavs in the army regret that they are going far from their ancestral homes and entering inhospitable lands from which many will not return, it being said openly that in the campaign of '48 the Shah was the more cunning general and that if it wasn't for the Sultan's guns his men would have stood no chance.

XVI

The reign of the present Sultan's father shone with justice. So writes a deputy judge and part-time dervish called Mevlana Isa in a new book in which he predicts the end of the world roughly forty-five years from now. Under Selim the sheep walked with the wolf and the mouse rested its head on the cat's paw. For all its worldly achievements, Mevlana concludes, for all its record of lawgiving, the reign of Suleyman has been tarnished by discord and greed.

When Suleyman conquered the Hungarian plain of Syrmia in 1526, he sent a chieftain and some judges to fetch Muslim tribes to settle there. But 'these [tribes] were not willing to be deported,' Mevlana recalls; 'they rebelled, they slew the chieftain and also killed the judges.' Each time the Sultan records a victory on the battlefield, his soldiers load up with so many slaves that the bottom falls out of the market and 'ten of them [do] not surpass the value of one'. As for the world's final hour, this will be heralded by a 'humiliation of the learned' when people listen keenly to fiddle music but ignore commentaries on the Quran.

Then there is the fantastic expense of it all. Take 1538, when Suleyman sent one armada to Gujarat and another to Prevesa while he himself led a huge army to Moldavia. Or the campaign of '48 which took tens of thousands of men off the land and cost him his silver plate. Or every year since Sinan became chief architect and started his programme of improvements, from a gigantic network of channels and aqueducts bringing water to Istanbul to the provision of covered markets across the Empire.

Would you believe that at this moment peasants are giving up their land having been crushed by Rustem's taxes and roam the hillsides in bands of twenty or more, teaming up with unemployed former religious students to ambush travellers? That the state's honoured couriers, who must be given food, a bed and fresh mounts wherever they go, trash caravanserais, seize the best horses which they ride to exhaustion and moonlight while still receiving an official salary; that the Sipahi cavalry abuse their position and extort from the people?

According to a recent French diplomatic report, 'out of obstinate insistence on achieving the goal of his enterprises, not only does [the Sultan] fall short of the fruit of his intentions but ... the forces of the said lord are feebler ... than at any time in the memory of men. His empire,' the report goes on, 'has always been considered so big and the number of his men and his horses that might be put in the field, so infinite, that were one or the other to be lost, whether in battle or by simple mortality, it would not be reckoned a notable reverse, and having lost one army he could just as easily raise another boasting as fine men and mounts. But now ... he is so short of soldiers and horses that he calls up palace boys as young as fourteen to make them Janissaries ... and there is a search for horses on all sides of the empire and such is the shortfall he takes the youngest colts.'

There is among the Sultan's subjects a growing tendency to doubt the sincerity of those in power, a suspicion that plots and machinations of a Machiavellian character are playing out in the shadows. Perhaps we are all, like Ibn Khaldun of Tunis, nostalgic for the days of the pioneer empire motivated by a love of God, a streaming banner and a raised sword.

~

When the state messenger arrives at Amasya with a letter instructing Mustafa to march south to join his father on the campaign, Mahidevran and Michiel the Venetian agree that it is a trap and that he must not go.

'Is it better to choose the empire of the world or a blissful life?' Mustafa asks his doctor of the law who replies that whoever owns the world experiences no happiness but is obliged to commit murders and other crimes and injustices. 'Those who know the brevity and fragility of this existence,' the man of God goes on, 'renouncing worldly vanity and nonsense . . . will be granted by God a place in the sky in which to enjoy eternally a blissful life.'

One night a magnificent prophet, dressed in the sun's rays, leads him by the hand to a rich and splendid palace set in a very pleasant garden. This place, the prophet tells him, houses all who lived virtuous lives, opposing injustice. Then he shows him an enormous river whose water is blacker than pitch in which a great number of people flail in agony. 'Here,' the prophet goes on, 'is the home of those great princes and kings and emperors who malignantly committed injustices while they were alive.' When he wakes up, the Prince relates his dream to the same doctor of the law who is afraid and begs him to have a care for his life.

On 6 October Mustafa steps onto the block from which it is his custom to mount his horse but it refuses to approach the block and successfully resists the efforts of the grooms and stewards to force it to do so. The Prince orders another horse to be brought forward, with the same result. Eventually he is obliged to mount from ground level and the party sets out uneasily and with foreboding, the destination being the marshy plain of Eregli, twenty farsakhs from the Cilician Gates that lead into Syria.

All the while, on the banks of the Bosporus, the Haseki waits for news and the people of the city, which has been entrusted to Rustem's brother, Sinan, presumably along with orders to take a hard line against pro-Mustafa sentiment, wait too.

~

When Rustem is informed that Mustafa is encamped near the army he orders the senior commanders to go to the Prince and offer him greetings. Then Rustem goes in a state of feigned perturbation to the Sultan and informs him that the commanders and Mustafa are plotting. Suleyman comes out of his tent and his jaundiced eye and corrupted judgement see further evidence of betrayal.

That same day an arrow lands at the edge of the Prince's camp carrying a message, purportedly from a friend: do not visit your father for you are in danger. Mustafa says that the arrow is the work of Rustem who wishes to provoke him into disobedience. And whether or not the arrow was fired by a provocateur, the Prince is indeed imprisoned in a circle of Rustem's making. To go to his father is to risk his life. Not to do so is to become a rebel.

His councillors beg him at least to meet the Sultan on open ground, on horseback and before the whole army. But a strange recklessness has come over Mustafa, it is as if he is challenging himself to exhibit to an excessive degree the innocence and virtue his enemies despise. Spurning his councillors he declares that he is unaware of having committed any harm against the Sultan, adding, 'if my father wishes to take my life, he will do so just as he gave it to me.'

Mustafa sends ahead presents including handsome horses and leather linings. He himself follows wearing a bulbous turban of the kind his father favours, a long robe of white and gold and a shirt of crimson satin, both he and his mount being in excellent order and most beautiful of aspect and form.

Arriving at the Sultan's tent city he dismounts and hands his reins to his steward. Entering the first tent he is met warmly by the Sultan's eunuchs and he unfastens his sword and leaves it there. Then he passes to the second tent, which is empty. At the entrance to the third tent the Sultan's gatekeeper tells him, 'wait, sire, you will enter presently.'

~

The Ottoman bow is related to the sacred bow of the Mongols. For the would-be bowman patience is essential. Damage your bow finger in youth and your career is over before it has begun. Hence the formative years of flexing a light practice bow and protecting the bow finger through the wearing of rings. The bow itself, made of sinew from the Achilles tendon of a buffalo stretched over a maple wand from Kastamonu, boiled, cooked over charcoal, glued using Danube resin, matured for a year and fed on linseed oil, will serve for two centuries. The horsehair bowstring is saturated in five parts beeswax, five parts resin and twenty parts fish glue, the flight guides are made of tortoiseshell or ivory, the arrow flights of swan, eagle or cormorant feathers and the shafts of pine and goat bone.

Sultan Suleyman sits holding his bow. He is crabbed from effort and suffering. He is dried up in old age, his beard has been left to grow, the nape of his neck is no longer smooth but wrinkled.

The Prince enters the tent and throws himself on the carpet before his father, the future genuflecting to the past, the possible to the tomb.

There is nothing wrong with the Sultan's eyesight. He sees the tents on the horizon, he sees the black-winged stilts among the reeds. Why, then, does he not see his unarmed son who has come to him in good faith, and lies prone and defenceless at his feet, but a traitor?

The Sultan is now capable only of the vituperative hatred that is reserved for one's own kith and kin. His eyes are coals, his lips are snakes, his heart is snares and thorns.

'Dog! Even now you have a mind to salute me?'

Kopek. An ugly word for an unclean animal.

Now the Prince feels the hand of the gatekeeper on him and hears the words, 'do not move, I do what I do by order of the Great Lord.' From the shadows three men come quickly forward, slipping a bowstring around his neck and pulling it so violently that the horsehairs tear and the Prince throws off the mutes and leaps up to make good his escape. And in truth all he needs to do is get out of the Sultan's tent and he will find not only his entourage but the whole Ottoman army that will protect him.

As the Prince runs for the door his feet catch in his robe and he pitches headlong onto the floor and the gatekeeper lunges for his leg and wraps himself around it. Now the mutes come for him with a second string and this time he jams his forearm between the string and his neck, also finding his voice and begging to have some few words with his father, just some few words to explain that he is not a traitor but a loving son. And it would cost the lawmaker little to order his eunuchs to sit on the Prince while he answers charges that have been laid against him by those who wish him ill and under a process that is destitute of law and propriety.

But Suleyman is no longer a lawmaker. He is an enraged and unreasonable tyrant and he shouts at the assassins, 'have you still not killed this traitor who for ten years did not let me have a restful night's sleep?' The Prince's turban is knocked off his head, exposing a cotton skullcap inscribed with talismanic formulae that protect the wearer from misfortune. His father orders it removed.

The second bowstring by now in shreds, a third is produced and wrapped around his neck and perhaps because he no longer benefits from occult protection, on this occasion the horsehairs hold and the Prince's grunts grow gradually fainter and his thrashing less vigorous and in this way while the mutes strain and heave and the Sultan sits holding his bow the life is squeezed from one who carried such hopes, who in common judgement surpassed in valour and goodness all other members of his house. And when the Prince lies still the gatekeeper rushes into the camp crying frenziedly and the Sultan has twenty-four hours to save himself and the Empire.

~

Let no one say he isn't clear-headed in a crisis even if it's one of his own making.

Michiel the Venetian and Mustafa's doctor of the law are immediately beheaded.

Rustem is relieved of his seal of office and the scapegoat slinks away leaving his tents flapping.

The Prince's obsequies are performed immediately and the corpse is sent to Bursa for burial.

The Janissaries are awarded a pay rise.

Men are ordered to Amasya to take Mahidevran and her grandson Mehmet away from that place and into exile at Gemlik on the Sea of Marmara.

~

Next the ambassador of the Shah is summoned and informed of the conditions for peace. The ambassador replies that he does not have the authority to conclude such an onerous peace accord and that he must return to his master for consultation. And the Sultan gives the order for the army to march through the Cilician Gates and into Syria to prepare for war.

The only element of Suleyman's clean-up operation that goes awry is his attempt to assuage the grief of Cihangir. Perhaps confusing his youngest son with one of his more bribable bureaucrats he tries to interest him in the governorate of Amasya and the possessions of his half-brother and the poor boy turns to him in agony and cries,

'Oh wicked chief, traitor, not a father!'

~

He marches into Syria, this man who has after decades of equivocation answered the question of how fair to fight, and how far, and must live with the consequences.

As his men march they mutter the poem that everyone is muttering:

O King of noble blood, is this your justice?
You may be lord of the world but is this grace?
Is this the practical wisdom of those who rule with judgement and
    skill?
You may be 'the lover,' but is this affection?
Is it tenderness to kill someone as dear to you as Mustafa?
You have been deluded by a lying trick and where is the truth in
    that?
You have been deluded by the words of an enemy: is that love?
You have shed his blood, is that the justice of a caliph?

In Istanbul, whether in the Muslim quarters of the imperial city or in Pera's Christian wards, it is impossible to go about one's business without hearing words of great regret and resentment from many mouths, particular odium being directed at Rustem, and there is expectation that some person will come forward from the ranks of the disgruntled to avenge himself of this dreadful crime, which has not only robbed the empire of its serenity but cut a path to further unnatural murders.

In his fifty-nine years Suleyman has known three solitary schemers, Ibrahim the Frank, Alvise Gritti and George Martinuzzi, but to scheme alone makes one drunk on one's own superiority and in the event all three met violent deaths. There is a second kind of schemer, the kind that looks for security in numbers. Hurrem knows that isolation is weakness and she has moved her pieces with skill. That said, the extended family she constituted with the aim of destroying Prince Mustafa will, regardless of its success in this endeavour, end up destroying itself. The mother clause insists on it.

~

At Gemlik after the dust has settled Mahidevran receives a visit from a eunuch of high rank who enquires after her wellbeing and that of her grandson Mehmet, and assures her that the Sultan is troubled by the death of Mustafa and that the author of this tragedy, Rustem, has been cast into disgrace. He tells her many stories of this kind, also presenting her with gifts and thus wins her confidence and trust. Then, drawing her attention to the confined atmosphere of the town, he obtains her consent to a change of air, and so they set out, Mahidevran in a carriage with her ladies and the eunuch and the Prince riding ahead.

Shortly into the journey the axle of Mahidevran's carriage snaps, arousing her suspicion, and she and her attendants are obliged to continue on foot. Far ahead, the Prince and the eunuch reach a house where the eunuch suggests that they rest and wait for the rest of the party. After crossing the threshold the Prince hears the words, 'the order of the Sultan is that you must die,' and when Mahidevran finally reaches the place she finds the body of her grandson, still warm with life.

Acknowledgements

My thanks to Cecilia Riva, Christina de Bellaigue, Jahan de Bellaigue, Rupert Walters, Nagihan Gur, the staff of the London and British libraries, Simon Shaps, Graeme Hall, Henry Howard, Stuart Williams, to my editor, Will Hammond, and my agent, Peter Straus.

Bibliography

Achard, Paul, *La Vie extraordinaire des frères Barberousse, corsaires et rois d'Alger*, Éditions de France, 1939

ad-Dabir, Abdullah Muhammad al-Makki al-Asafi al-Ulughkhani Hajji, *An Arabic History of Gujarat*, trans. M.F. Lokhandawala, Oriental Institute, 1970

Ağca Diker, Sevgi, 'Has Oda ve Teskilati', doctoral thesis, Istanbul University, 2019

Ak, Coşkun (ed.), *Muhibbi Divani*, (2 vols), Trabzon Valiliği Yayınları, 2006

Alberi, Eugenio (ed.), *Le relazioni degli ambasciatori veneti al Senato durante il secolo decimosesto* (18 vols), Società editrice fiorentina, 1839–1863

Anonymous, *Viaggio et impresa che fece Soleyman Bassa del 1538 contra Portoghesi per racquistar la Citta di Diu in India*, Venice, 1543

Atcil, Muhammet Zahit, 'State and Government in the Mid-Sixteenth Century Ottoman Empire: The Grand Vizierates of Rustem Pasha (1544–1561)', doctoral thesis, University of Chicago, 2015

Atil, Esin, Suleymannameh: *The Illustrated History of Suleyman the Magnificent*, National Gallery of Art, Washington DC, 1986

Aubin, Jean, 'Études Safavides I. Sah Ismail et les Notables de l'Iraq persan', *Journal of the Economic and Social History of the Orient*, vol. 2, no. 1, Jan. 1959

Ayalon, David, *Outsiders in the Lands of Islam*, Variorum Reprints, 1988

Baer, Marc David, *Khans, Caesars and Caliphs*, Basic, 2021

Barnes, Jonathan, *The Complete Works of Aristotle*, Princeton University Press, 1984

Bassano, Luigi, *Costumi et i modi particolari della vita de'Turchi*, Institut fur Gesichte und Kultur des Nahen Orients an der Universitat des Nahen Orients, Max Hueber, 1963

Bayraktar, Nimet, 'Semsi Ahmed Pasa, Hayati ve Eserleri', *Tarih Dergisi*, vol. 33, 1982, pp. 99–114

Bechet, A., *Histoire du ministère du cardinal Martinusius*, Paris, 1715

Berindei, Mihnea, and Veinstein, Gilles, *L'Empire ottoman et les pays roumains, 1544–1545*, Éditions de l'École des hautes études en sciences sociales, 1987

Berthoud, Gabrielle, et al., *Aspects de la propagande religieuse*, E. Droz, 1957

Bourilly, V-L., *Le journal d'un bourgeois de Paris sous le règne de François Ier (1515–1536)*, Alphonse Picard, 1910 [1]

Bourilly, V.-L., *Lettres écrites d'Italie par François Rabelais*, Librairie de la société des études Rabelaisiennes, 1910

Bouvier, Yann, *Antoine Escalin des Aimars (1498?–1578); le parcours d'un ambassadeur de François Ier*, Recherches Alpes-Maritimes et contrées limitrophes régionales', no. 188, 2007

Breton, Françoys, de Rincon, Antoine, Cantelmo, Joachin, Cantelmo, Cesare, and Bourilly, V.-L., 'Les diplomates de François Ier. Antonio Rincon et la politique orientale de François Ier (1522–1541)', *Revue Historique*, vol. 113, fasc. 2, 1913, pp. 268–308

Busbecq, Ogier Ghiselin, *Lives and Letters*, trans. Charles Thornton Foster and F.H. Blackburne Daniell (2 vols.), C. Kegan Paul and Co., 1881

Çabuk, Vahit (ed.), *Divan-ı Muhibbi (Kanuni Sultan Süleyman'ın Şiirleri)*, Tercüman, 1980

Casale, Giancarlo, *The Ottoman Age of Exploration*, Oxford University Press, 2010

Celalzade, Mustafa, *Selim-name*, ed. Ahmet Uğur and Mustafa Çuhadar, Kültür Bakanlığı, 1990; repr. Millî Eğitim Bakanlığı, 1997

Celalzade, Mustafa Çelebi, *Kanuni'nin Tarihçisinden Muhteşem Çağ*, Kariyer, 2011

Centorio degli Hortensi, Ascanio, *Commentarii della Guerra di Transylvania*, Venice, Gabriel Gioliti de Ferrari, 1566

Çerçi, Faris, *Haberleşme Hizmetleri ve Osmanlı Devlenti'nde Ulak Organizasyonu*, Atatürk Üniversitesi İlahiyat Fakültesi Dergisi, no. 20, 2003

Charrière, E. (ed.), *Négociations de la France dans le Levant*, vol. 1, Imprimerie nationale, 1848

Chesneau, Jean, *Voyage de Paris en Constantinople*, Droz, 2019

Clot, André, *Suleiman the Magnificent*, trans. Matthew J. Reisz, Saqi, 2012

Coutinho, Lopo de Sousa, *Historia do Cerco de Diu*, Bibliotheca Classicos Portuguezes, 1890

Crespin, Jean, *Histoire des martyres*, vol. 1, Société des livres religieux, 1885

de Bellaigue, Christopher, *The Lion House*, The Bodley Head, 2022

de La Roncière, Charles, *Histoire de la marine française*, Plon, 1899

Denison Ross, E., 'Gujarat and Khandesh', in Haig, Wolseley (ed.), *The Cambridge History of India*, vol. 3, S. Chand and Co., 1965

Denny, Walter B., *Iznik: The Artistry of Ottoman Ceramics*, Thames and Hudson, 2004

Deny, Jean, and Laroche, Jane, 'L'expédition en Provence de l'armée de mer du Sultan Suleyman sous le commandement de l'amiral Hayreddin Pacha dit Barberousse (1543–1544)', *Turcica*, vol. 1, 1969, pp. 161–211

Dernschwam, Hans, ed. Hans Hattenhauer and Uwe Bake, *Ein Fugger-Kaufmann im Osmanischen Reich. Bericht von einer Reise nach Konstantinopel und Kleinasien 1553–1555 von Hans Dernschwam*, Peter Lang, 2012

Džaja, Srećko M., and Weiss, Günter (eds), *Austro-Turcica 1541–1552, Diplomatsiche Akten des hapsburgischen Gesandtschaftswerkerhrs mit der Hohen Pforte im Zeitalter Süleymans des Prächtigen*, R. Oldenbourg, 1995

Faria y Souza, Manuel de, *The Portugues Asia* (trans. John Stevens), London, C. Brome, 1695

Finkel, Caroline, *Osman's Dream: The Story of the Ottoman Empire 1300–1923*, Basic Books, 2005

Fischer, Erik, *Melchior Lorck*, vol. 4: *The Constantinople Prospect*, trans. Peter Spring and Dan Marmorstein, The Royal Library, Vandkunsten Publishers, 2009

Fleischer, Cornell, 'Alqas Mirza', *Encyclopaedia Iranica*, vol. 1, fasc. 9, 1989, pp. 907–9: http://www.iranicaonline.org/articles/alqas-alqasb-alqas-mirza-safawi (accessed 2 July 2024)

Fodor, Pál (ed.), *The Battle for Central Europe: The Siege of Szigetvár and the Death of Süleyman the Magnificent and Nicholas Zrínyi (1566)*, Brill, 2019

Forrer, Ludwig, *Die osmanische Chronik des Rustem Pascha*, Mayer & Muller, 1923

Freely, John, *Jem Sultan: The Adventures of a Captive Turkish Prince in Renaissance Europe*, Harper Collins, 2004

Gachard, Louis (ed.), *Collection des Voyages des souverains des Pays-Bas*, 4 vols, F. Hayez, 1874–82

Garnier, Édith, *L'Alliance impie: François Ier et Soliman le Magnifique contre Charles Quint (1529–1547)*, Éditions de Felin, 2008

Geuffroy, Antoine, *Briefve description de la court du grand turc*, Paris, 1546

Gökbilgin, M. Tayyib, 'Rüstem Paşa ve Hakkındaki İthamlar', *Tarih Dergisi*, vol. 8, nos 11–12, 1956, pp. 11–50

Goodwin, Godfrey, *The Janissaries*, Saqi Essentials, 1994

Guboğlu, M., 'L'inscription turque de Bender relative à l'expédition de Soliman le magnifique en Moldavie (1538/945)', *Studia et Acta Orientalia*, vol. 1 (1957), 1958

Guiffrey, Georges (ed.), *Cronique du Roy Françoys premier de ce nom*, Libraire de la société de l'histoire de France, 1860

Guilmartin, John Francis, Jr, *Gunpowder and Galleys: Changing Technology and Mediterranean Warfare at Sea in the Sixteenth Century*, Cambridge University Press, 2004

Güngör Şahin, Hüseyin, *İspanyol ve Osmanlı Kaynaklarına Göre Barbaros Hayreddin Paşa*, Panama Yayincilik, 2019

Gürkan, Emrah Safa, *Sultanın Korsanları: Osmanlı Akdeniz'inde Gaza Yağma ve Esaret, 1500–1700*, Kronik, 2018

Giovio, Paolo, *La prima parte dell'istorie del suo tempo*, (trans. Lodovichi Domenichi), Venice, Giovan Maria Bonelli, 1560

Hammer-Purgstall, J. de [von], *Histoire de l'Empire Ottoman*, trans. J.J. Hellert, vols 5 & 6, Bellizard, Barthes, Dufour et Lowell, 1836

Heyd, Uriel, 'Moses Hamon, Chief Jewish Physician to Sultan Süleymān the Magnificent', *Oriens*, vol. 16, 1963

Hughes, Bethany, *Istanbul: A Tale of Three Cities*, Weidenfeld and Nicolson, 2017

Hüsameddin, Abdi-Zade Hüseyin, *Amasya Tarihi*, Amasya Belediyesi, 1986

İğdemir, Uluğ (ed.), *Kanunî Armağanı*, Türk Tarih Kurumu Basıimevı, 1970

İnalcık, Halil, *The Ottoman Empire: The Classical Age 1300–1600*, Weidenfeld and Nicolson, 1997

İnalcık, Halil, *An Economic and Social History of the Ottoman Empire, 1300–1600*, Cambridge University Press, 1997

İnalcık, Halil, and Kafadar, Cemal (eds), *Süleymân the Second and his Time*, Isis, 1993

İpşiroğlu, Mazhar Ş., *Masterpieces from the Topkapı Museum: Paintings and Miniatures*, Thames and Hudson, 1980

Isom-Verhaaren, Christine, *Allies with the Infidel: The Ottoman and French Alliance in the Sixteenth Century*, I.B. Tauris, 2011

Jurien de La Gravière, Jean Pierre Edmond, *Doria et Barberousse*, Librairie Plon, 1886

Karaback, Josef von, *Zur orientalischen Altertumskunde*, vol. 7 (*Geschichte Suleimans des Grossen, verfasst und eigenhandig geschrieben von seinem Sohne Mustafa*), Kais. Akademie der Wissenschaften in Wien, 1917

Kırzıoğlu, M. Fahrettin, *Osmanlilar'in Kafkas-Elleri'ni fethi, 1451–1590*, Türk Tarih Kurumu, 1993

Knecht, R.J., 'Francis I and Paris', *History*, vol. 66, no. 216, 1981, pp. 18–33

Knecht, R.J., *Francis I*, Cambridge University Press, 1982

Kuran, Aptullah, *Sinan: The Grand Old Master of Ottoman Architecture*, Institute of Turkish Studies, 1987

Kurtoğlu, Fevzi, 'Hadım Süleyman Paşa'nın Mektupları ve Belgradın Muhasara Plânı', *Belleten*, vol. 4, issue 13, 1940, pp. 53–88

Laski, Hieronymus, 'Tagebuch des Hieronymus Laski wahrend seiner zweiten Gesandtschaft bei Sultan Suleyman', in A. von Gévay, *Urkunden und Aktenstücke zur Geschichte der Verhältnisse zwischen Oesterreich, Ungarn und der Pforte im XVI und XVII Jahrhunderte*, Schaumburg, 1842, pp. 1–68

Lellouch, Benjamin, *Les ottomans en Égypte. Historiens et conquérants au XVIe siècle*, Peeters, 2006

Levy, Avigdor, *The Jews of the Ottoman Empire*, Darwin Press, 1994

Lowry, Heath, 'From Trabzon to Istanbul: The Relationship between Suleyman the Lawgiver and his Foster Brother (*Süt Karındaşı*) Yahya Efendi', *The Journal of Ottoman Studies*, vol. 10, 1990

Luther, Martin, *Works of Martin Luther*, trans. C.M. Jacobs, vol. 1, A.J. Holman Company, 1915, repr. Project Gutenberg, 2010: https://www.gutenberg.org/cache/epub/31604/pg31604-images.html (accessed 2 July 2024)

Machiavelli, Niccolo, *The Prince*, trans. Tim Parks, Penguin, 2009

Marozzi, Justin, *Baghdad: City of Peace, City of Blood*, Allen Lane, 2014

Maurand, Jérôme, *Itinéraire de Jérôme Maurand d'Antibes à Constantinople*, trans. Léon Dorez, 1892

Membre, Michele, *Mission to the Lord Sophy of Persia (1539–1542)*, trans. with introduction A.H. Morton, School of Oriental and African Studies, University of London, 1993

Menavino, Giovanantonio, *I cinque libri della legge, religione, et vita de'Turchi*, 1548

Monshi, Eskandar Beg, *History of Shah 'Abbas the Great* (Tārīkh-e 'Ālamārā-ye 'Abbāsī), trans. Roger M. Savory, Westview, 2 vols, 1978

[Murat, Seyyid,] *Barbaros Hayreddin Paşa – Gazavâtnâmesi ve Zeyli*, ed. Abdullah Gündoğdu, Hüseyin Güngör Şahin and Dilek Altun, Panama Yayıncılık, 2019

Murphey, Rhoads, *Ottoman Warfare 1500–1700*, UCL Press, 1999

Navai, Abdolhossein, *Shah Tahmasp Safavi: Majmu'e-ye Asnad va Mukatebat-e tarikhi hamrah ba Yaddashtha-ye tafsili*, Entesharat-e Bonyad-e Farhang-e Iran, n.d.

Necipoğlu, Gülru, *Architecture, Ceremonial and Power: The Topkapi Palace in the Fifteenth and Sixteenth Centuries*, Architectural History Foundation, 1991

Necipoğlu, Gülru, *The Age of Sinan*, Reaktion, 2005

Nordman, Daniel, *Tempête sur Alger. L'Expédition de Charles Quint en 1541*, Éditions Bouchène, 2011

Nuntiaturberichte aus Deutschland nebst erganzenden Aktenstucken (1533–1559), Deutsches Historisches Institut in Rom, 1892

Orhonlu, C., 'Khadim Süleyman Pasha,' *The Encyclopaedia of Islam*, vol. 4, E.J. Brill, 1978

Parker, Geoffrey, *Emperor: A New Life of Charles V*, Yale University Press, 2019

Paruta, Paolo, *Degl'istorici delle Cose Veneziane*, Venice, 1718

Peçevi, İbrahim Efendi, *Tarih*, Kultur Bakanlığı Yayınları, 1981

Peirce, Leslie P., *The Imperial Harem: Women and Sovereignty in the Ottoman Empire*, Oxford University Press, 1993

Peirce, Leslie P., *Empress of the East: How a European Slave Girl became Queen of the Ottoman Empire*, Basic Books, 2017

Penzer, N.M., *The Harem*, Spring Books, 1966

Porter, Venetia (ed.), *Hajj: Journey to the Heart of Islam*, British Museum Press, 2012

Possevino, Antonio, *Transylvania* (1584), Tipografia Artistica Stephaneum, 1913

Pujeau, Emmanuelle, 'Preveza in 1538: the background of a very complex situation', Second International Symposium on the History and Culture of Preveza, Sep 2009, Preveza, Greece. pp. 121–38: https://hal.science/hal-00833534 (accessed 2 July 2024)

Rajyagor, S.B., *History of Gujarat*, S. Chand and Co., 1982

Reston, James, *Defenders of the Faith: Christianity and Islam Battle for the Soul of Europe, 1520–26*, Penguin, 2009

Rogers, J.M., and Ward, R.M., *Suleyman the Magnificent*, British Museum Publications, 1988

Roper, Lyndal, *Martin Luther: Renegade and Prophet*, The Bodley Head, 2016

Rumlu, Hasan Beg, *Ahsan al-tawarikh*, trans. C.N. Seddon, Oriental Institute, 1934

Ruscelli, Girolamo, *Lettere di principi, le quali ò si scrivono, da principi, ò à principe, ò ragionan di principi*, Venice, Giordano Ziletti, 1564

Şahin, Kaya, *Empire and Power in the Reign of Süleyman*, Cambridge University Press, 2013

Saint-Genois, M. le Baron, and Yssel de Schepper, G.-A., *Missions diplomatiques de Corneille Duplicius de Schepper*, Académie royale de Belgique, 1856

Sanuto, Marino, *Diarii*, 58 vols, Deputazione di Storia Patria per le Venezie, 1872–1902

Savory, Roger, *Iran Under the Safavids*, Cambridge University Press, 1980

Scheurl, C., *Einrit Keyser Carlen in die alten kayserlichen haubstatt Rom, den 5 Aprilis, 1536*, Nuremberg, Christoph Scheurl, 1536

Schutte, Anne Jacobson, *Pier Paolo Vergerio: The Making of an Italian Reformer*, Travaux d'Humanisme et Renaissance, no. 160, Droz, 1977

Sebag Montefiore, Simon, *Jerusalem: The Biography*, Weidenfeld and Nicolson, 2011

Servantie, Alain, *Raisons à faire paix plutôt que guerre. Charles-Quint et Soliman*, Isis, 2020

Setton, Kenneth M., 'Lutheranism and the Turkish Peril', in *Balkan Studies*, vol. 3, 1962, pp. 133–68

Setton, Kenneth M., *The Papacy and the Levant (1204–1571)*, 4 vols, The American Philosophical Society, 1984

Sigonio, Carlo, *Della vita et fatti di Andrea Doria, principe di Melfi*, trans. Pompeo Arnolfini, Genoa, Giuseppe Pavoni, 1598

Silay, Kemal (ed.), *An Anthology of Turkish Literature*, Indiana University Press, 1996

Solak-zâde, Mehmed Hemdemî Çelebi, *Solak-zâde Tarihi*, ed. Vahid Çabuk, Kültür Bakanlığı, 1989

Staffetti, Luigi, *La politica di papa Paulo III e l'Italia (a proposito d'una recente pubblicazione)*, Archivo Storico Italiano, series 5, vol. 33, no. 233, 1904

Sumner-Boyd, Hilary, and Freely, John, *Strolling through Istanbul*, Sev Yayıncılık, 1997

Taner, Melis, 'Power to Kill: A Discourse of the Royal Hunt during the Reigns of Suleyman I and Ahmed I', MA thesis, Sabancı University, 2009

Tezcan, Semih, *Bir Ziyafet Defteri*, Simurg, 1998

Tommaseo, M.N. (ed.), *Relations des ambassadeurs vénitiens sur les affaires de France au XVIe siècle*, vol. 1, Imprimerie royale, 1838

Turan, Serafettin, *Kanuni Sultan Süleyman Dönemi Taht Kavgaları*, Kapı, 2011

Uğur, Ahmet (ed.), *Asafnâme* (Lütfi Paşa), Kultur ve Turizm Bakanlığı Yayınları, 1982

Uluçay, M. Çağatay (ed.), *Osmanlı Sultanlarına Aşk Mektupları*, Ufuk, 2001

Ursu, J., *La Politique orientale de François I (1515–1547)*, Honoré Champion, 1908

Utiešenović, O., *Lebensgeschichte des Cardinals Georg Utiešenović genannt Martinusius*, Wilhelm Braumüller, 1881

Uzunçarşılı, İsmail Hakkı, 'Sancağa Çıkarılan Osmanlı Şehzadeleri', *Belleten*, vol. 39, no. 159, 1990, pp. 659–96

Vandenesse, Jean de, *Collection des voyages des souverains des Pays-Bas*, ed. [Louis Prosper] Gachard, vol. 2, F. Hayez, 1874

Villegaignon, Nicolas Durand de, *Relation de l'expédition de Charles-Quint contre Alger*, trans. Pierre Tolet, Auguste Aubry, 1874

Wilson, Jean D., and Roehrborn, Claus, 'Long-Term Consequences of Castration in Men: Lessons from the Skoptzy and the Eunuchs of the Chinese and Ottoman Courts', *The Journal of Clinical Endocrinology and Metabolism*, vol. 84, no. 12, 1999, pp. 4324–31

Zarinebaf-Shahr, Fariba, 'Qizilbash "Heresy" and Rebellion in Ottoman Anatolia during the Sixteenth Century', *Anatolia Moderna*, vol. 7, 1997, pp. 1–15

Notes

Chapter I

5 here is the King: Tommaseo, 279

5 purest ... part of Christendom: Knecht (1982), 139

5 one of his sons: Bourilly (1910 [1]), 357

5 bolder by the year: Ursu, 86

6 put him to heavy expense: Tommaseo, 67

6 execrable blasphemy: Berthoud et al., 115

6 false antichrists: Berthoud et al., 117–19

6 burned alive at the cemetery of Saint-Jean: Crespin, 302

6 a crowd outside Notre Dame: Berthoud et al., 112

7 on suspicion of being German: Bourilly (1910 [1]), 358

7 the Blessed Sacrament is what they shall have: Guiffrey, 114

7 a pole apiece: Knecht (1982), 250

8 skin the colour of watery milk: Knecht (1982), 83

8 this is his intention: Knecht (1982), 250

8 pleasures and self-interest: Setton (III), 404

9 plumper than the portraits: Schutte, 95

9 a German drunk: *Nuntiaturberichte* (I/I), 542

10 their master and prophet: *Nuntiaturberichte* (I/I), 541; Schutte, 94–5

10 all the wine the Tiber can carry: Bourrilly (1910), 38

10 a clear run in: Bourilly (1910), 58

10 obscenely wealthy: Bourilly (1910), 56

11 his objective is the Duchy of Milan: Ursu, 182

11 fall into enmity: Vandenesse, 122

11 the Pope on Easter Day: Parker, 247

12 the feet and hands of the Pope: Charriere (I), 297

12 his sister Eleanor: Vandenesse, 124

12 with great reluctance: Vandenesse, 123

12 he would gain Milan: Knecht (1982), 296

Chapter II

Chapter III

Chapter IV

Chapter V

66 and to the glory of God: Necipoglu (2005), 117
66 must not favour one over another: Necipoglu (2005), 272
66 female attendants and eunuchs: Necipoglu (2005), 44
66 haircuts and shoes: Necipoglu (2005), 273
66 vinegar and a little pepper: Dernschwam, 165

Chapter VI

69 put his brothers to death: Inalcik (1997), 59
70 was also strangled: Mikhail, 245
70 dead or alive: Pierce (1993), 50
70 triple spots in yellow: Rogers and Ward, 167
71 something called grammar: Rogers and Ward, 86–7
71 the easy informality of a boy: Pierce (2017), 202
71 Menavino's travelogue: Ulucay, 43
71 this twelve-year-old: Pierce (2017), 202
71 help themselves to whatever they want: Dernschwam, 159
72 lodged in the tree behind: Taner, 24
72 and from the Grand Turk: Menavino, 11
73 embraced and kissed tenderly: Menavino, 245
74 adorned with jewels: Sanuto (LIII), 451–2
74 as he has seen his father do many times: de Bellaigue, 121
75 spending his mother's allowance: Pierce (1993), 49
75 Konya is somewhere in between: Alberi (series 1, III), 76–7
75 already taller than his father: Dernschwam, 180
75 sparse and blond to thick and dark: Membre, 9
75 a most pleasing sight: Sanuto (LVII), 632
75 fifteen-year-old son: Uzuncarsili (1975), 685
76 their ladies-in-waiting: Peirce (1993), 46
76 the elements of divine prosperity: Ulucay, 255
76 bans him from the pulpit: Husameddin, 122
77 the bucolic side of his personality: Husameddin, 27
77 a good work–life balance: Ulucay, 255
77 he needed to guard against: Peirce (1993), 78
77 noble and blessed grace: Ulucay, 256
77 further from the capital: Charriere (I), 497
77 used to be Opukovic: Agca Diker, 19
78 the Sultan's sword-holder: Alberi (series 1, III), 98
78 piety, politeness and sobriety: Necipoglu (2005), 297
78 So answers Hurrem: Atcil, 38–9
79 suffers from the French disease: Casale, 87
79 the Sultan's only daughter: Atcil, 40
79 seven hundred inmates: Dernschwam, 157
79 markets of Tahtakale: Forrer, 103
79 rice and flax go to cinders: Dernschwam, 159
79 one hundred and thirty children: Hammer-Purgstall (V), 304
79 from Second to Grand: Ugur, 3

Chapter VII

81 their aversion cools: Tommaseo, 230
81 surpassing even King Francis: Gayangos, *Calendar of State Papers* (V/I), no. 206
82 to convince him to relent: Gachard et al., 156
82 the decorations on his route: Knecht (1982), 296
82 until it is time for bed: Parker, 265
82 will be crowned Emperor of Constantinople: Charriere (I), 390
82 started his career in Charles's household: Setton (III), 315
83 as if I had come from heaven: Setton (III), 252
83 the grandeur of France: Ursu, 134–5
83 the porter a few coins: Charriere (I), 479–80
83 but only an intermission: Ursu, 118
83 making Milan over to his son Philip: Parker, 267
83 except by cutting it off: Ursu, 121
84 excruciating in a famine: Setton (III), 451
84 which I am told can be captured easily: Parker, 271
84 to vanquish, not to be vanquished: Parker, 271–2
84 from which he raids the coasts of Spain: Parker, 272
85 a French diplomat familiar with proceedings: Charriere (I), 430
85 penchant for vomiting devils: Roper, 381
85 the Pope is a liar and the Turk a murderer: Setton (III), 151
85 sent by God to try his people: Setton (III), 141
85 contributions to the common defence: Setton (III), 460
85 capable of liberating Constantinople: Setton (III), 167
85 God protect me from this gracious lord: Setton (III), 149
86 Hungary's first king: Giovio, 551
86 will reign over Hungary: Hammer-Purgstall (V), 324; Utiesenovic, 55
86 in return for an annual tribute: Charriere (I), 445
86 free to serve whomsoever we will: Laski, 8–9
87 establish a better friendship: Laski, 5
87 besieging Queen Isabella and her infant in Buda Castle: Hammer-Purgstall (V), 324
87 trying to deceive me: Laski, 11
87 taken away to prison: Dzaja, 116
87 to lift the siege of Buda: Pecevi, 164
87 pending a full-scale invasion: Laski, 11
88 to make war against . . . the Emperor: Ursu, 167
88 Fregoso, a Genoese noble: Garnier, 194
88 wobbling along the bridle paths: Charriere (I), 505
88 travel through the night: Parker, 278
88 the ambassadors are intercepted: Charriere (I), 506
88 kept under worse conditions: Charriere (I), 506
89 becoming his godfather: Parker, 272
89 the missing men: Parker, 280
89 he knows nothing of their whereabouts: Parker, 508
89 from the creation of the world until now: Parker, 283

Chapter VIII

Chapter IX

Chapter X

114   reduced to making peace: Garnier, 220
114   flying French colours: Garnier, 221
115   the pirate king has his queen: Garnier, 221
115   on the Lutheran question: Parker, 294
115   caring nothing for their name or honour: Giovio, 694
115   he will become a Christian: Setton (III), 470
115   typically French unpreparedness: Garnier, 224
115   and Charles not far away with his: Garnier, 225
116   to accept his surrender: Giovio, 726
116   and into the Turkish camp: Giovio, 726
116   clemency and good treatment: Giovio, 727
116   wine rather than cannon balls: Giovio, 727
116   to fly south: Charriere (I), 566
117   gurgling to the bottom: Giovio, 729
117   to kill off Andrea Doria: Giovio, 729
118   the fine town of Toulon: Deny and Laroche, 181
118   no Christian state is excluded: Charriere (I), 559
118   a regrettable feature of Christian navies: Joncieres, 386
119   bewitches whoever beholds it: Deny and Laroche, 180–81
119   more lambs . . .: Charriere (I), 572–3
119   enduring many travails: Charriere (I), 570
120   two hundred thousand quintals: Garnier, 231
120   off the coast of North Africa: Garnier, 232
120   as much an enemy of Christendom as the Turk himself: Garnier, 233
120   a hateful memory of himself: Giovio, 768
121   eight hundred thousand ecus: Garnier, 235
121   accompany him with his five ships: Joncieres, 390
121   but less moody: Giovio, 770
121   points him towards Suez: Giovio, 770
121   damaging his lands there: Giovio, 771
122   the ancient Greeks and Romans before them: Giovio, 773
122   the doubtful storms of uncertain autumn: Giovio, 773
122   the honour and affection due a father-in-law: Giovio, 686
122   to which they are exposed: Bouvier, 86–7
123   produces delicious raisins: Maurand, 105
124   gall has many useful qualities: Maurand, 129
124   in the presence of the husband: Maurand, 127
125   suppress Lutheranism in Germany: Knecht (1982), 370–71
126   powder and munitions: Maurand, 203
126   oblige him to execute marvellous leaps: Maurand, 189
126   destined for the next India campaign: Maurand, 201
126   of England, Holland and Venice: Maurand, 199
127   to be deflowered: Schepper, 130

Chapter XI

129   might as well belong to another building: Necipoglu (2005), 196
130   keep snake numbers down: Maurand, 229
130   the mighty arches were set in heaven: Sumner-Boyd and Freely, 41
130   crocus-gold from Libya and Tyrian purple: Hughes, 223

Chapter XII

151   wrap up with an orgy: Membre, xvi–xvii
151   Safi al-Din's mausoleum in Iran: Inalcik (1997), 196
152   alcohol, hashish and sodomy: Membre, xvi
152   is expected any time now: Membre, xxiv
152   four thousand such migrants at Tabriz: Zarinebaf-Shahr, 8
153   to the province of Iraq: Membre, 18
153   become captive to the heretics: Cabuk, 425
153   acquire worldly possessions: Cabuk, 494
153   a great commentary on the Quran: Hammer-Purgstall (VI), 4
153   they must be executed: Necipoglu (2005), 53
153   the basis of Ottoman law: Necipoglu (2005), 35
154   the present Sultan's grandfather: Servantie, 58
154   king of Shirvan: Monshi (I), 115
154   the Sultan is out of town: Pecevi (I), 191
154   the Prince addresses a letter: Fleischer
154   on the heads of kings: Navai, 170
155   if you tend to me: Navai, 172
155   a cannibal eunuch: Hammer-Purgstall (VI), 7
155   and embraces Sunnism: Fleischer
155   they will flock to me: Monshi (I), 120
155   the Prince is a wreck: Hammer-Purgstall (VI), 8
155   the palate of the cannibal eunuch: Tezcan, 7–29
156   lovingly sewn her royal brother: Pecevi (I), 192
156   punished by mighty God: Pecevi (I), 193
156   to announce the forthcoming campaign: Topkapi Palace collection, Istanbul
156   On 8 April: Celalzade (2011), 272
156   determined by his astrologer: Dzaja, 229
156   to Uskudar and the waiting army: Celalzade (2011), 273–4
157   for trial and punishment: Zarinebaf-Shahr, 10–12
157   What they avoid mentioning: Sahin, 116
157   Selim in Phrygia: Dzaja, 229
157   his own blood-stained succession: Kirzioglu, 183
157   oversexed and usually hungover: Alberi (series 1, III), 116
158   he will kill you all: Alberi (series 1, III), 77
158   and the Safavids in turn: Sahin, 121
158   to kiss a king's passing hand: Chesneau, 50
158   put the red-headed ones to the sword: Celalzade (2011), 276
158   taking and retaking from each other: Chesneau, 50
158   all the way to Tabriz: Chesneau, 51
158   There is nothing to eat: Savory, 62
158   five thousand horses, camels and mules: Rumlu, 149
159   massacre or enslavement: Hammer-Purgstall (VI), 11
159   retrace their steps to Van: Chesneau, 54
159   using ropes of hemp: Celalzade (2011), 277–8
159   the Sultan's possessions: Monshi (I), 120
159   hang copper vessels: Pecevi (I), 197
159   in terror and confusion: Hammer-Purgstall (VI), 12
159   alongside the Turks: Pecevi (I), 198
160   and Khurasan carpets: Hammer-Purgstall (VI), 13
160   sedition, rebellion, and bloodshed: Monshi (I), 194
160   thrown from the ramparts: Fleischer

Chapter XIII

171 spread out of malice: Dzaja, 399
172 The Sultan and Rustem aren't talking: Dzaja, 563
172 He has a bunion: Dzaja, 565
172 a grace-and-favour apartment or two: Knecht (1962), 423

Chapter XIV

173 deserve certain condemnation: Charriere (II), 132
173 treasurer and chief justice: Utiesenovic, 68
174 danced hoodless: Utiesenovic, 69
174 royal residence at Krakow: Utiesenovic, 58
174 sending the entire Treasury to [Ferdinand]: Dzaja, 520
174 the provincial capital, Alba Iulia: Charriere (II), 128
174 the Pasha is put to flight: Setton (IV), 566
175 the Queen bursts into tears: Utiesenovic, 845
175 than it is to Alba Iulia: Setton (IV), 567
175 to pass on to his master: Centorio, 88
175 ISABELLA REGINA: Centorio, 88
176 Italian and Bohemian troops: Utiesenovic, 88–9
176 wouldn't say no to a cardinal's hat: Charriere (II), 568
176 to drive away the Hapsburgs: Utiesenovic, 104
176 overlooking the Bosporus: Hammer-Purgstall (VI), 21
176 to take both his neighbour's: Utiesenovic, 103
177 to save us from the common danger: Hammer-Purgstall (VI), 27
177 the left bank of the Mures: Centorio, 93
177 brought the glad tidings a few days ago: Setton (IV), 571
177 twelve hundred Turks lie dead: Centorio, 129
177 on the opposite bank: Centorio, 130
177 the fortress above the town: Centorio, 132
177 to their deaths in the ditch below: Centorio, 130
177 drinking their horses' blood: Centorio, 132
178 benevolent and clement: Centorio, 134
178 to hand triumph to your enemies: Centorio, 136
178 four war horses: Setton (IV), 574
179 less to forestall a large-scale invasion than to encourage one: Setton (IV), 576
179 diet of Transylvanian nobles: Setton (IV), 575
179 I do not wish him to leave it alive: Utiesenovic, 134
179 are in a frenzy to get in: Centorio, 144
180 twenty-five strongholds: Setton (IV), 585

Chapter XV

187 built himself a memorial mosque: Inalci and Kafadar, 64
187 the Hungarian city of Pressburg: Dernschwam, 120
188 the walls that encircle the city: Sebag Montefiore, 293
188 the Queen of Sheba: Necipoglu (2004), 190
188 refugees from Hapsburg persecution: Sebag Montefiore, 293
188 night journey to heaven: Peirce (2017), 289
188 whose fortunes looked up: Peirce (2017), 291

Chapter XVI

204   covered markets across the Empire: Necipoglu (2005), 315
204   crushed by Rustem's taxes: Turan, 19; Ruscelli, 167
204   ride to exhaustion: Cerci, 211
204   takes the youngest colts: Charriere (II), 97–8
205   enjoy eternally a blissful life: Ruscelli, 169
205   have a care for his life: Ruscelli, 170
205   that lead into Syria: Alberi (series 1, III), 208
206   evidence of betrayal: Ruscelli, 170
206   provoke him into disobedience: Alberi (series 1, III), 208–9
206   just as he gave it to me: Alberi (series 1, III), 209
206   unfastens his sword and leaves it there: Alberi (series 1, III), 210
207   shafts of pine and goat bone: Goodwin, 82
207   no longer smooth but wrinkled: Igdemir, 301
208   a restful night's sleep: Ruscelli, 170
208   other members of his house: Alberi (series 1, III), 210
208   leaving his tents flapping: Alberi (series 1, III), 213
211   still warm with life: Busbecq (I), 120–22

Index

Christ Chalkites, 129
Christianity, 15
   Catholicism, 5–12, 84–5, 116, 141
   Lutheranism, 6–10, 84–5, 125,
      140–41, 142, 164, 176
   Ottoman subjects, 156–7
   relics, 7, 131
Church of St Mary, Buda, 93–4
Cicek, 70
Cihangir, Şehzade, 70, 135, 156, 158,
   168, 200, 209
Cilician Gates, 205, 209
circumcision, 73, 85, 94, 109
Clement VII, Pope, 10
Cleopatra VII, Queen of Egypt, 25
clocks, 142
Columbus, Christopher, 26
Column of Arcadius, Istanbul, 64–5
Commissary, 22, 23
Constantinople, see Istanbul
Corfu, 13–15, 38, 39, 41, 44
Cornwall, England, 37
Cortes, Hernan, 99
Council of Trent (1545–63), 141
Covered Market, Istanbul, 143, 167
Crepy Accords (1544), 125, 142, 145
Crete, 38, 39
Crimean Khanate, 46
Croatia, 91
Crown of St Stephen, 175
Crown of Thorns, 7
Crusades, 5, 7
Csepel, Hungary, 93
Curzola, 37
Cyprus, 143
Cyrus II, King of Persia, 24

Da Gama, Vasco, 26
Da Silveira, Antonio, 32
Dalmatia, 113
Danube River, 44, 45, 93, 176
Dardanelles, 84
Davud Pasha, 78
De la Garde, Antoine des Aimars,
   Baron, 113–17, 119, 122
Dimetoka, Thrace, 69, 111, 172, 191,
   195
Diu, Gujarat, 27, 30–34, 92, 95, 203

Diyarbakir, Syria, 78, 79, 163
Dniester River, 46, 134
Dome of the Rock, Jerusalem, 188
Doria, Andrea, 36–42, 83, 98–9,
   101–2, 117, 120, 126
Doria, Giannettino, 123
Doria, Lamba, 37

earthquakes, 64–5
Easter, 11
Ebussuud Efendi, 153–4, 169–70,
   199, 201
Edirne, Thrace, 44, 155, 157, 168,
   171, 194
Egypt, 17, 25, 26, 27–9, 78, 87, 121,
   133, 165, 189
Elba, 121
Elbe River, 164
Eleanor, Queen consort of France, 81
elephants, 19, 47, 144
Enghien, Francis de Bourbon, Count,
   115, 116
England, 9, 35, 37, 61, 126, 137, 144
Enver (eunuch), 57
Erasmus of Rotterdam, 5
Eregli, Anatolia, 205
Erzincan, Anatolia, 159
Erzurum, Anatolia, 158, 192, 193–4,
   196
Esztergom, siege of (1543), 135
Etampes, Anne d'Heilly, Duchess, 81,
   172
eunuchs, 24–6, 57
Euphrates River, 158
Eve, 29
Eyup, 58, 153

falconry, 19, 22, 86, 87
Fenandez, Anne, 32, 33
Ferdinand, Archduke of Austria, 36,
   43, 83–6, 140, 141, 161
   Janos, agreement with (1538), 173,
      174
   Siege of Buda (1541), 87, 92, 96,
      114
   succession, 164, 172
   Transylvanian campaign (1551),
      174–80

Christopher de Bellaigue is the award-winning author of *The Lion House: The Rise of Suleyman the Magnificent*, which was chosen as a book of the year by *The Times, Sunday Times, Spectator* and *New Yorker* among others, as well as five previous books, including *The Islamic Enlightenment*, which was shortlisted for the Baillie Gifford Prize for Non-fiction and the Orwell Prize for Political Writing in 2017.

As a reporter he has covered war, politics, society and the environment on five continents for *The Economist*, the *New York Review of Books*, the *Guardian* and the BBC. He is the founder of the Lake District Book Festival in Cartmel, Cumbria, an Honorary Fellow of the University of St Andrews and in 2026 he will take up a Visiting Fellowship at All Souls College, Oxford.

www.christopherdebellaigue.com